VISUAL JOURNAL

VISUAL JOURNAL

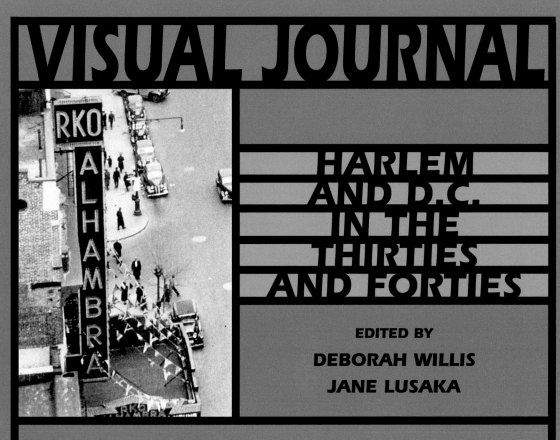

HARLEM AND D.C. IN THE THIRTIES AND FORTIES

EDITED BY

DEBORAH WILLIS

JANE LUSAKA

THE CENTER FOR AFRICAN AMERICAN HISTORY AND CULTURE

AND

SMITHSONIAN INSTITUTION PRESS

WASHINGTON AND LONDON

©1996 by the Smithsonian Institution
All rights reserved

Editor: Catherine F. McKenzie
Production Editor: Jack Kirshbaum
Designer: Kathleen Sims

Library of Congress Cataloging-in-Publication Data
Visual Journal: Harlem and D.C. in the thirties and forties /
edited by Deborah Willis and Jane Lusaka; with essays by Jane Freundel Levy . . . [et al.].
        p.   cm.
Includes bibliographical references (p.).
ISBN 1-56098-691-3
1. Documentary photography—New York (N.Y.)—History—20th
century. 2. Documentary photography—Washington (D.C.)—
History—20th century. 3. Afro-Americans—New York (N.Y.)—
History—20th century—Pictorial works. 4. Afro-Americans—
Washington (D.C.)—History—20th century—Pictorial works.
5. Harlem (New York, N.Y.)—History—20th century—Pictorial works.
6. Washington (D.C.)—History—20th century—Pictorial works.
I. Willis-Thomas, Deborah, 1948- II. Lusaka, Jane.
TR820.5.V57 1996
973' .0496073—dc20   95-49656

British Library Cataloging-in-Publication data available

Manufactured in the United States of America
00 99 98 97 96   5 4 3 2 1

Printed on recycled paper. ∞ The paper used in this publication meets the minimum requirements of the
American National Standard for Permanence of Paper for Printed Library Materials Z39.48-1984.

For permission to reproduce any of the illustrations, please correspond directly with the sources.
The Smithsonian Institution Press does not retain reproduction rights for these illustrations individually
or maintain a file of addresses for photo sources.

To the photographers—
Robert H. McNeill,
Gordon Parks,
Morgan and Marvin Smith,
and Addison, Robert, and George Scurlock—
who collectively created
a comprehensive record of African American life
during a pivotal time in American history.

CONTENTS

FOREWORD

In every society there are persons who have the responsibility of recording or committing to memory the history of a people. These individuals have been called scholars, griots, elders, historians, chroniclers, keepers of the torch. Their accounts have been told and retold by famous as well as unfamous storytellers. Personal accounts of a people's collective history have been written in pictographic and hieratic script; they have been drawn on the walls of caves, carved into gourds and trees, written on papyrus and bark, stitched into clothes, etched onto stone, and printed on rag paper.

Each generation revisits these stories and images for the purpose of establishing connections with the past and expanding their sense of continuity. From studying these images and stories, a young viewer might learn that three thousand years ago young Egyptian women had their hair dressed and braided in a manner similar to that of young African American women today. One might also view old newspaper clippings and family photographs to confirm an affinity with more recent ancestors: Does he resemble his grandmother? Does she share a talent with her father? Is he continuing a social, political, or spiritual tradition for which his family has been known?

Visual Journal: Harlem and D.C. in the Thirties and Forties focuses on the works of seven contemporary griots who used photography to chronicle the lives of African Americans in two distinct urban communities: Washington, D.C., and New York City. These images capture the daily activities of working people, as well as extraordinary events that united and bonded individuals into a cohesive whole. The photographers documented the toils of historically significant leaders, in some instances while they were still being groomed for leadership. They recorded African Americans engaged in acts of devotion and conflict, during triumphs and tragedies; and they have encouraged viewers to be discerning as they gaze retrospectively at opportunities lost and visions that have been fulfilled.

Every community values certain achievements. In the African American community the impediment of the color barrier created opportunities for many individuals to achieve status as the "first" person in their community to enter into a world that was previously off-limits. The documentation of experiences related to desegregation are not to be taken lightly, for these individuals often were abused for taking on the responsibility of showing the white community that competency and intellect are not matters of color.

Many who were first, and who spoke up with the knowledge that retribution might be forthcoming, were leaders in an effort to uplift the race. The victory of one was considered to be the victory of many. Everyday people became symbols of triumph and role models for the larger group. Successful athletes, entertainers, entrepreneurs, and city workers provided the black masses with viable models for obtaining the American dream.

While *Visual Journal: Harlem and D.C. in the Thirties and Forties* documents individual achievement, it also illustrates the so-called separate but equal society that African Americans created. These photographers documented weddings, debutante balls, lodge events, political rallies, union meetings, parades, and dinners honoring local, community, and national leaders. A people who were omitted from celebrations and commemorations by the larger society found solace in their own inventions.

The fallacy of the separate but equal society was embedded in economics. Whereas African Americans created organizational structures that mirrored their counterparts in the white community, African American fiscal resources were limited and their community institutions were never well endowed. Nonetheless, what the community lacked in fiscal resources, it made up with creativity. African American seamstresses and tailors dressed the growing upper middle class; community-based restaurateurs catered and hosted important events; and the black press documented these events for their readers and posterity.

Robert H. McNeill; Gordon Parks; Addison, Robert, and George Scurlock; and Morgan and Marvin Smith were invited to the most memorable parties. They covered political rallies and important events and documented the lives of individuals who made a difference in their communities. *Visual Journal: Harlem and D.C. in the Thirties and Forties* encourages each of us to look back at a moment in history when American blacks believed in the American dream. They pursued the dream, fought for the right to participate in the democratic process, mourned their losses, celebrated their victories, and created new visions for a brighter future.

Claudine K. Brown
Director of Arts
Nathan Cummings Foundation
Former Project Director
National African American Museum Project

ACKNOWLEDGMENTS

Thank you to our fellow authors, Jane Freundel Levey, Nicholas Natanson, and Melissa Rachleff, who contributed such wonderful essays to this project. We extend our gratitude to Robert H. McNeill, who generously provided us with images from his personal collection, and to Gordon Parks, Vivian E. Scurlock, Monica Smith, and Marvin Smith, who granted us permission to use photographs from their respective collections at the Moorland-Springarn Research Center at Howard University, the Library of Congress, and the Schomburg Center for Research in Black Culture. Special thanks to the many organizations and individuals who provided cooperation, advice, and support during the production process: Susan McNeill, Maricia Battle, Oggi Ogburn, Donna Wells, Cary Beth Cryor, Lucien Aigner, Ildiko De Angelis, and the archives staff at the National Museum of American History, as well as our colleagues at the Center for African American History and Culture: Steven C. Newsome, Shireen L. Dodson, Toni Brady, Deirdre Cross, Elanna Haywood, Suzanne Pilet, Shirley Solomon, and Mark Wright.

VISUAL JOURNAL

1. INTRODUCTION

Deborah Willis

In the following lighthearted passage from Langston Hughes's *The Best of Simple*,[1] the fictional character Jesse B. Simple poignantly places the black photographer in the black community and shows black people in a picture-taking mode. It also reveals Simple's consciousness of the lack of representation of identifiable black images on radio and television.

It was a warm evening not yet dark when I stopped by Simple's. His landlady had the front door open, airing the house, so I did not need to ring. I walked upstairs and knocked on his door. He was sitting on the bed, cutting his toenails, listening to a radio show, and frowning.

"Do you hear that?" he asked. "It's not about me, nor about you. All these plays, dramas, skits, sketches, and soap operas all day long and practically nothing about Negroes. You would think no Negroes lived in America except Amos and Andy. White folks have all kinds of plays on the radio about themselves, also on TV. But what have we got about us? Just now and then a song to sing. Am I right?"

"Just about right," I said.

"Come on, let's go take a walk." He put on his shoes first, his pants, then his shirt. "Is it cool enough for a coat?"

"You'd better wear one," I said. "It's not summer yet, and evening's coming on. You probably won't get back until midnight. . . ."

It was dusk-dark when we reached the pavement. Taxis and pleasure cars sped by. The Avenue was alive with promenaders. On the way up the street we passed a photographer's shop with a big sign glowing in the window:

HARLEM DE-LUXE PHOTOGRAPHER STUDIO
IF YOU ARE NOT GOOD-LOOKING
WE WILL MAKE YOU SO
ENTER

"The last time I come by here," said Simple, "before my lady friend started acting like an iceberg, Joyce told me, 'Jess, why don't you go in and get your picture posed? I always did want a nice photograph of you to set on my dresser.'

"I said, 'Joyce, I don't want to take no picture.' But you know how womens is! So I went in. They got another big sign up on the wall inside that says:

RETOUCHING DONE

"I don't want them to 'touch' me, let alone 'retouch,' I told Joyce.
"Joyce said, 'Be sweet, please, I do not wish no evil-looking Negro on my dresser.' So I submitted.
"Another sign stated:

COLORED TO ORDER—EXPERT TINTING

"I asked, 'Joyce, what color do you want me to be?'
Joyce said, 'A little lighter than natural. I will request the man how much he charges to make you chocolate.'"[2]

In the 1930s and 1940s, in cities all over America, photography studios—like the one Hughes imagines in his Simple stories—explored, documented, and reinforced the common culture within African American communities. Members of the black public were enthusiastic about having their images preserved at the local studio. They enshrined their local photographers, who, encouraged by the numerous requests for photographs, became prominent fixtures on the social circuit.

Photographers illustrated exceptional versatility as they recorded the lives and activities of political, entertainment, sports, and intellectual figures such as Adam Clayton Powell Jr., Marian Anderson, Joe Louis, the Negro Baseball League players, Mary McLeod Bethune, and Charles Drew. Their works ranged from dynamic street photography to stylized portraiture. Today, their images encourage us to view—and review—our community histories in creative and insightful ways.

Museum educator Deborah Klochko has written:

> What is photography? Today, it is hard to pin a label on the medium—it can be a single image taken by a camera and printed on sensitized paper. It can be drawn upon, enlarged, cut, reassembled or it can be a series that supports an idea. It can be an installation that can be experienced by direct participation. It is almost impossible to singularly describe photography—it can be so many things.

For me, photography is participatory, sometimes active, oftentimes passive. Photographers are my visual storytellers. Photography has been a part of my consciousness since 1955, when I first saw the book, *The Sweetflypaper of Life,* by Langston Hughes and photographer Roy DeCarava. For me and my family, photographs attested to our place in society, documented our dreams, and preserved powerful memories. Cultural critic bell hooks recalls the consciousness of the camera:

> The camera was the central instrument by which blacks could disprove representations of us created by white folks. . . . For black folks, the camera provided a means to document a reality that could, if necessary, be packed, stored, moved from place to place. It was documentation that could be shared, passed around. And, ultimately, these images, the worlds they recorded, could be hidden, to be discovered at another time.[4]

In 1972, I began a search to find those hidden photographs that bell hooks mentions in the above passage. My search led me to public and university libraries, scholars' and family bookshelves, discarded magazines and newspapers with titles like *Flash!, Our World, Messenger, Opportunity, Crisis, Bronze, Ebony/Jet, Silhouette Pictorial, Negro Digest, New York People's Voice, Life,* and *Look.* I found unfamiliar names like Morgan and Marvin Smith; Robert H. McNeill; Addison, Robert, and George Scurlock; and one recognizable name—Gordon Parks! There were many others such as Moneta

Sleet Jr., Winifred Hall Allen, Roy DeCarava, and Frank Cloud. Eleven years later, I published a bio-bibliography of black photographers, listing references and other sources of information on black photographers active in this country since 1840. My purpose—then and now—is to expand our perspective of the activities of African American photographers, to rediscover our dreams and our memories. Whereas a complete history of photography is still unwritten, *Visual Journal: Harlem and D.C. in the Thirties and Forties* offers another footnote in the photographic canon.

This volume of essays and photographs examines a specific body of work executed between 1929 and 1949 by seven visual storytellers, some of whom had formed family businesses and partnerships: Gordon Parks, Morgan and Marvin Smith, Robert H. McNeill, and the Scurlocks—Addison, Robert, and George. It speaks to the cultural perspectives these photographers brought to their work and the individual communities they documented: New York City's Harlem, Washington, D.C., and nearby rural Virginia. These photographers were more than detached observers, they were participants; their images resonate with compassion and honesty. The photographers are linked by the uniqueness of their vision and the understanding that they were recording their diverse and distinctive communities at a critical time in American history.

The 1930s was a highly charged political time. It witnessed the depression, President Franklin D. Roosevelt's New Deal program, Jim Crow laws, and the Great Migration. The 1940s experienced a world war, which conversely brought a sense of hope and opportunity to the entire American public. As Henry Louis Gates Jr. so eloquently suggests, during the Great Migration,

> African Americans reinvented themselves, as more than a million souls removed themselves from the provinces to the metropole, from the periphery to the center, from South to North, from agriculture to industrial, from rural to urban, from the nineteenth century to the twentieth. The greatest transformation of all, of course, was a "new" Negro culture, the outcome of the exchange of traditional southern and northern black cultures and the resulting synthesis of the two.[5]

Visual Journal looks at the world of black America during this transformation. For a community in the midst of reinventing itself, photographs were crucial; they documented African American achievements as well as despair in a segregated society. By the mid 1930s, smaller handheld cameras and faster films helped photographers to express their discontentment with social conditions and to document day-to-day events, social activities, children at school and at play, and men and women at work. This period also witnessed the beginning of street photography and the documentation of public pageantry and events. Simultaneously, the federal government—on a limited basis—began to make a visual record of the African American experience. Gordon Parks worked for the Farm Security Administration, and Robert H. McNeill for the Works Progress Administration Writers Project—both programs a part of President Roosevelt's New Deal.[6]

The work of the seven photographers studied in this volume reveal the photographers' sense of race consciousness and racial intervention. As Gordon Parks stated, "I learned to fight the evil of poverty—along with the evil of racism—with a camera."[7] The images presented in *Visual Journal* can be used as a basis for critical discussion as we begin to carefully reconstruct the period in which they were made. As James Baldwin so aptly noted, black people needed witnesses in this hostile world.

Four of *Visual Journal's* contributors—Melissa Rachleff, Jane Lusaka, Nicholas Natanson, and Jane Freundel Levey—discuss and reconsider the imagination and vigilance of these photographers who produced work under the complexities of making a living and creating art in a segregated society. My chapter on Gordon Parks is a further exploration of historical and biographical notions in the world of photography. These essays fill a gap in a project that began some fifty years ago. As Sally Stein and Pete Daniel state:

> [T]he FSA had no monopoly on New Deal photography. In 1936, Time Inc. conducted a survey of available sources of picture material as part of the groundwork of putting together *Life* magazine, that preeminent vehicle for thirties photography. On returning from an out-of-town reconnaissance mission, a staff picture researcher announced to her New York colleagues that Washington was the center of the photographic field. In the nation's capital could be found foreign photo collections maintained by embassies and every major archive of the federal government.[8]

Documentary photographs by black photographers, however, were overlooked by the survey. I hope that the essays in *Visual Journal* will encourage the reader to imagine the narrative of each photographer as he discovers the streets of Harlem or Washington, D.C., or the dusty roads of Virginia—and to revisit these cities through photography.

Melissa Rachleff opens with an overview of the importance of the journalistic photography of Morgan Smith and his twin brother, Marvin. The Smiths, born in 1910 (Morgan died in 1993), were two of Harlem's leading photojournalists and studio photographers in the 1930s and 1940s. Their second-floor studio, M. Smith Studio, was located next to the famous Apollo Theater on 125th Street. It was frequented by performing artists, writers, and historians. Their cameras captured the rallies as well as the breadlines and street corner orators of the depression. They photographed black nationalists on one corner and black socialists on another.

In Harlem, the Smiths found a newly migrated, working-class, educated black clientele that included writers, religious leaders, politicians, and visual and performing artists. As Arna Bontemps writes of his own first days in Harlem:

> From the window of a small room in an apartment on Fifth and 129th Street I looked over the rooftops of Negrodom and tried to believe my eyes. What a city! What a World! And what a year for a colored boy to be leaving home the first time! Twenty-one, 16 months out of college, full of golden hopes and romantic dreams, I had come all the way from Los Angeles to find the job I wanted, to hear the music of my taste, to see serious plays and, God Willing, to become a writer. The first danger I recognized that fall, however, was that Harlem would be too wonderful for words. Unless I was careful, I would be thrilled into silence.[9]

No doubt the Smith twins, when they arrived in New York at the age of twenty-one, experienced similar emotions as newcomers to the community (Fig. 1.1).

The Smith brothers experienced a lifetime of collaborative projects. Much of their early work was published in the *New York Amsterdam News* and the *New York People's Voice*. Their studio was popular among families and church groups, and both brothers were interested in culture and politics.

Jane Lusaka's essay offers the reader an insightful overview of Robert H. McNeill's photography in Washington, D.C. During the 1930s and 1940s, McNeill, born in 1917, created a comprehensive documentary record of African American life in Washington (Fig. 1.2). Frequently working on a free-lance basis, McNeill took photographs of the Washington, D.C., metropolitan area that appeared regularly in the prominent African American newspapers and magazines of the era—the *Pittsburgh Courier, Washington Afro-American, Chicago Defender,* and *Washington Tribune,* among others. "It was a natural, human interest thing," remembers the photographer. "[The newspapers] were looking for pictures of people and they were trying to increase circulation. . . . I was busy all the time."[10] McNeill's photographs document that African Americans living in a segregated capital city

1.1 Morgan and Marvin Smith, *Bird's Eye View of Seventh Avenue, Harlem*, n.d. Schomburg Center for Research in Black Culture, New York Public Library.

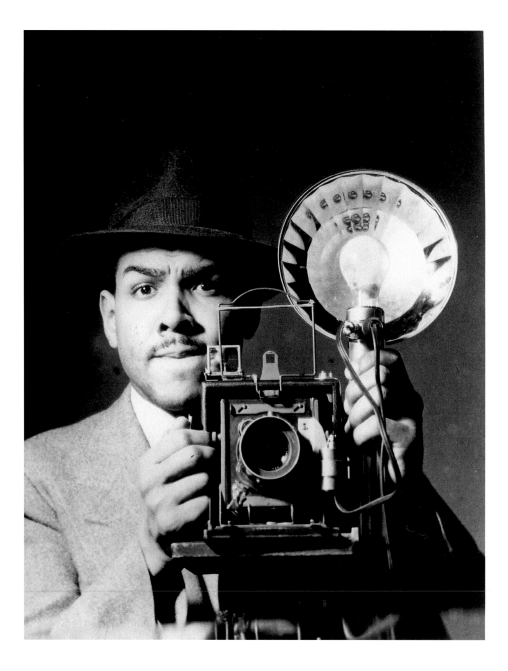

1.2 Robert H. McNeill, *Self-Portrait*, 1940s. Courtesy of Robert H. McNeill, Washington, D.C.

survived—even thrived—by creating their own social and community structures and religious and cultural organizations.

Nicholas Natanson examines McNeill's photography of black communities in Virginia, produced while he was working with the Works Progress Administration Federal Writers' Project. Some of these photographs were featured in *The Negro in Virginia*, published in 1940; it marked the first photographic and historical survey of African American life in that state. Natanson also reads into the context of published journalistic images of black women looking for work on a New York City street corner in a series that became known as the *Bronx Slave Market*. In a wonderfully comprehensive essay, Natanson affirms McNeill's photography of the period.

Jane Freundel Levey discusses the impact of Addison Scurlock's photography in the early twentieth century, particularly on his sons, Robert and George. Addison Scurlock (1883–1964) opened his first studio on U Street in Washington, D.C., in 1911. When both sons were high school students, they apprenticed with their father, receiving extensive training in portrait photography under his direction. While Addison did a substantial amount of studio photography, Robert (1917–1994) and George (1919–) were drawn to news photography (Fig. 1.3). Their journalistic photographs appeared in black newspapers such as the *Washington Afro-American, Philadelphia Tribune, Pittsburgh Courier, New York Amsterdam News, Norfolk Journal-Guide*, and *Chicago Defender*. At the same time, Robert was on assignment for the black picture magazines *Our World, Flash!*, and *Ebony*.

During the 1940s, Scurlock Studios worked diligently to increase the visibility of black intellectuals, artists, musicians, and politicians in the Washington D.C., area. The studio also documented community life: activities at Howard University, conventions and banquets, sorority and social club events, dances, weddings, cotillions, and local business affairs. In 1948, Robert and George established the Capitol School of Photography, where they paid homage to their father's legacy by training young photographers.

My essay examines the images of Washington, D.C., made by Gordon Parks (1912–). These images speak of the another black Washington, not found in the photographs of the Scurlock Studios and Robert McNeill. Parks draws our attention to effects of racism and provides us with a candid investigation of poverty and isolation, hope and the duality of life, in pre–World War II Washington (Fig. 1.4).

The theme of this volume and exhibition exemplifies the mission of the Center for African American History and Culture, which was established for the purpose of documenting, preserving,

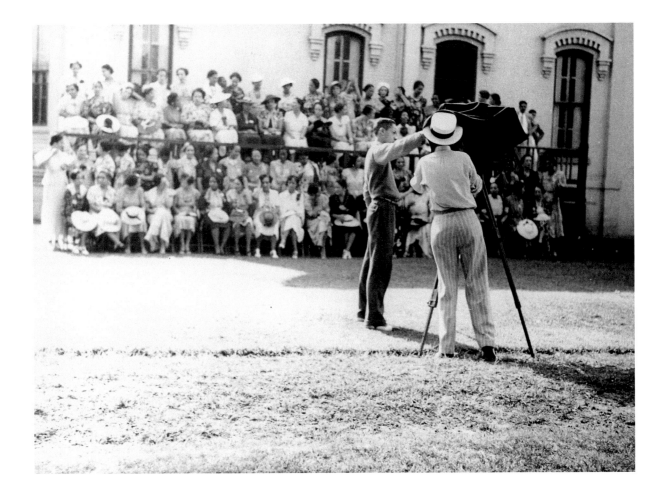

1.3 Robert H. McNeill, *Addison and George Scurlock Photographing a Howard University Event,* 1930s. Courtesy of Robert H. McNeill, Washington, D.C.

1.4 Gordon Parks, *Neighborhood Children, Southwest Washington, D.C.*, November 1942. Library of Congress, LC-USF 3-10074-G.

and interpreting the full range and breadth of experiences of people of African descent in the United States and throughout the diaspora. These photographs of social life, political events, and everyday experiences also correspond to the theme of the Smithsonian Institution's 150th anniversary celebration, which "highlight[s] the unique work of the Smithsonian . . . in research, collections, exhibitions, publications, education and public programs [and reflects] Smithsonian concerns for conserving the diversity of cultural life."[11]

The essays herein provide a sensitive reading into photography in the 1930s and 1940s. Expanding on the concept of race-conscious imagery, seven visual storytellers documented the well- and lesser-known black men, women, and children of Washington, D.C., New York, and Virginia. These photographers empowered their communities, and the past lives again through their work.

Notes

1. Jesse B. Simple of Harlem was one of Hughes's best-loved fictional characters. As the Simple tales grew in number and were assembled periodically in book form, they ultimately filled four volumes. Langston Hughes explained that "it is impossible to live in Harlem and not know at least a hundred Simples, fifty Joyces." Quoted in Abraham Chapman, ed., *Black Voices* (New York: St. Martins Press, 1970), p. 97.

2. Langston Hughes, "Picture for Her Dresser," in *The Best of Simple* (New York: Hill and Wang, 1961), p. 106.

3. *California Museum of Photography Biennial I*, exhibition catalog (Riverside: California Museum of Photography, University of California, Riverside, 1989), p. 2.

4. bell hooks, "In Our Glory: Photography and Black Life," in *Picturing Us: African American Identity in Photography*, ed. Deborah Willis (New York: New Press, 1995), p. 48.

5. Henry Louis Gates Jr., "New Negroes, Migration, and Cultural Exchange," in *Jacob Lawrence: The Migration Series* (Washington, D.C.: Rappahannock Press in association with the Phillips Collection, 1993), p. 19.

6. During the depression, the U.S. government established many social assistance programs and agencies. In 1935, Rexford Guy Tugwell, who was to become a close advisor to Franklin D. Roosevelt, set up the Resettlement Administration to extend aid to farmers. In 1937, the agency was absorbed by the Department of Agriculture and renamed the Farm Security Administration (FSA).

"The New Deal Program set up a number of . . . projects, each with different administrations, goals, and constituencies. . . . The largest and most famous of these, the Works Progress (later Work Projects) Administration . . . was active from 1935 through 1943." Merry A. Foresta, "Art and Document: Photography of the Works Progress Administration's Federal Art Project," in *Official Images: New Deal Photography*, ed. Pete Daniel and Sally Stein (Washington, D.C.: Smithsonian Institution Press, 1987), p. 148.

7. Martin H. Bush, *The Photographs of Gordon Parks*, exhibition catalog (Wichita, Kans.: Edwin A. Ulrich Museum of Art, Wichita State University, 1983), p. 50.

8. Daniel and Stein, eds., *Official Images: New Deal Photography*, p. viii.

9. Jervis Anderson, *Harlem: The Great Black Way, 1900–1950* (London: Orbis Publishing, 1982), p. 142.

10. Robert H. McNeill, interview with Jane Lusaka, March 14, 1995.

11. "Smithsonian Institution 150th Anniversary Steering Committee Report," Smithsonian Institution internal memo, August 1994, p. 11.

2. PHOTOJOURNALISM IN HARLEM

MORGAN AND MARVIN SMITH AND THE CONSTRUCTION OF POWER, 1934–1943

Melissa Rachleff

Photography had a massive impact upon American culture during the Roosevelt era, from 1933 to 1945. During this period, photography was embraced by the federal and state governments, political groups, businesses, artistic movements. In sum, all branches of society began implementing the documentation of their activities on a massive scale.[1] Photographic organizations either sprang up or received new life. One of them was the Photo League in New York, a group that trained people from all backgrounds to document their lives and workplaces. The underlying mission of this photographic activity was to alleviate the nation's anxiety over the failure of the "American way of life" caused by the greatest economic depression in U.S. history.[2] During the Roosevelt years, photographers sought to locate and make visible an American culture that could not only survive the economic crisis but rise above it.

Yet 1930s photography was not solely linked to social conditions. Coinciding with the depression were a series of technological advancements in cameras and film, in particular the Speed Graphic and the 35 mm Leica. These handheld cameras made photography portable and thus made possible the cultivation of a genre of urban street photography and, concurrently, the documentary style exemplified in the government-sponsored projects.[3] (The Farm Security Administration, or FSA, became synonymous with this approach.) These new modes in photographic coverage proliferated throughout the print media.

Photographic historians have recently turned to this dynamic period to uncover marginalized histories. In particular, studies of African American representation and photography offer a different perspective from which to more fully understand American life in the 1930s.[4] Yet scant attention has been paid to the photographs taken by African American photographers for an African American audience. Instead, most studies have based their assessment of these obscured histories on photographs taken by well-known white photographers or from the famous documentary projects. As Angela Davis noted, the most valorized images of black life "have incorporated the vision of white artists, necessarily outsiders to the culture from which their images were taken. From the era of photography's emergence up to the present period, black photographers have been rendered—forcibly and systematically—invisible."[5]

One reason for the lack of critical scholarship on African American photographers is that most were banned from working in the major media. This was effected in practice if not in official policy. Oral testimonies attest to active racist policies devised to keep black and immigrant workers out of the mainstream press.[6] The major press, representing the interests of an Anglo-American power structure, reflected its biases as well. Most often, then and continuing to the present time, if African American life was represented in the dominant media, it was shown as devastated and crime ridden.

These discriminatory practices, however, did not entirely stifle the development of an African American photojournalism during the 1930s. By employing African American photographers, the extensive network of the black press—one of the traditional sites of resistance to white hegemony—became the major forum for contesting the negative imagery proliferating through the dominant media. The photographs published in the black press constituted a response to the dominant ideology that saw all African Americans as inferior to white society. More than that, the photographs functioned as a way of building an identity that a mass black audience could relate to and, significantly, support.

In Harlem the twin-brother photographers Marvin and Morgan Smith made visible the key issues and events that were facing African Americans during the depression and war years (Fig. 2.1). The Smiths virtually invented a modern photojournalist practice through their photographs taken for the black press, in particular the *New York Amsterdam News* and the *People's Voice*. The Smiths produced a large body of work indicative of the subject matter covered by the black press during that period—

society, entertainment, politics, crime—and, later, portraits and advertisements from the commercial portrait studio they ran from the 1940s through the 1950s.[7] This essay examines a small but crucial area of the Smiths' career, their photojournalist practice for the black press, centering on their photographs of boxer Joe Louis, an international figure, and, during the 1940s, the pastor and congressman Adam Clayton Powell Jr. How the papers utilized the Smiths' work and what control they exercised in cultivating their profession will also be considered.

Biographical Background

Morgan Smith was one of Harlem's leading photojournalists from 1934 through the early 1950s, and became the *Amsterdam News*'s first staff photographer in 1937. Along with his partner and twin, Marvin, he operated one of Harlem's most popular commercial portrait studios, the M. Smith Studio, which was located next to the Apollo Theater on 125th Street from 1939 through the 1950s.

The Smiths arrived together in New York during the height of the depression in 1933 when they were twenty-one years old. Deciding not to take advantage of their college football scholarships, the Smiths left Kentucky to pursue a fine arts career in Harlem, "because we had friends graduating from the leading [black] colleges and coming back to no jobs, doing the same work we were."[8] At that time Harlem had a reputation as a leading cultural center, a legacy left over from the Harlem Renaissance period of the 1920s.

In Harlem the Smiths found great poverty, with 50 percent of its residents unemployed (by conservative estimates).[9] Unlike those that had left the South only a few years earlier seeking economic advancement, the Smiths went to Harlem seeking social and cultural enrichment. With little money, but luckily having obtained work on the first of the government work projects (Civil Works Administration), the Smiths found in Harlem an opportunity to develop creatively through institutions like the YMCA, the 135th Street branch of the New York Public Library, and, importantly, Augusta Savage's open-studio classes (Fig. 2.2).[10] In 1936 Morgan Smith was hired as an artist apprentice on the federal mural projects under the Federal Arts Project (FAP), working under painter Vertis Hayes at Harlem Hospital.

The Smiths also discovered a black bourgeoisie, essentially a college educated, middle-class group who organized and participated in cultural and social activities.[11] This group, with its connections to literature, art, and entertainment, was radically different from anything the Smiths had experienced in the South. Indeed, the black bourgeoisie was the inspiration behind the popular culture represented in the black press. Key artistic figures—writers such as Claude McKay and Langston Hughes (Fig. 2.3), entertainers like Duke Ellington and Ella Fitzgerald (Figs. 2.4 and 2.5), and the actress and activist Fredi Washington (Fig. 2.7)—were representative of the broad range of cultural life that flourished in Harlem. The Smiths' social and cultural interests coincided with those of the black bourgeoisie and thus with the editorial focus of the black press as well. In focusing on diverse and talented individuals, the black press—and ultimately the Smiths—turned away from photographic reportage of poverty. This editorial position sharply contrasted with the reportage in the mainstream press. The documentary style had emerged as the signature approach of the depression era, characterized by the representation of the bleak social conditions throughout the South and the northern inner cities. Yet the black press was not formed for the purpose of depicting abject conditions; its mission was rather to cultivate resistance to the racist society and to educate, inspire, and entertain its readership.

Whereas the Smiths were partners throughout much of their lives—even marrying twin sisters in a double wedding in 1936, then divorcing both in 1939—this essay focuses on the photojournalistic work of Morgan Smith. During their professional careers, in and out of photography, the Smiths always shared a credit line: "M & M Smith." As Morgan Smith later stated, "I insist on giving credit to Marvin and Morgan Smith. It could have just been M. Smith."[12] Further, it is Morgan Smith who is listed as staff photographer at both the *Amsterdam News* and *People's Voice* newspapers, though Marvin always provided crucial emotional and practical support. In 1938, when the Smiths opened their first commercial studio, the photography became more of a collaboration.

Morgan Smith began working as a photojournalist for the *Amsterdam News* when a friend, a cartoonist at the paper, suggested he submit a photograph of the Harlem Easter parade. That first photograph might have been one that appeared on April 7, 1934, as a front-page picture depicting smartly dressed twin sisters. Twins would have naturally interested Smith as a subject. The photograph is a full-length society portrait, most likely posed, and framed by painted lines. Illustrative framing was a common device in newspaper practice, stemming from the turn of the century.[13] Such designs were employed to make the subject more elegant, giving the snapshot the high-quality look of a studio portrait.

The society section was, commercially, the newspaper's most important section. It added glamour and prestige, distinguishing itself from the competition by the social figures it represented. The editorial embellishments were most likely thought to add a refinement to the candid street portraits Smith routinely submitted to the paper. The design of the society section also indicates the paper's uneasiness about using candid snapshots to represent members of society. This discomfort might have been related to a snapshot's most common subject in news reporting—the urban street—a subject made common by the Speed Graphic camera, widely adopted and used also by Smith. Street photographs embodied everyday life with an immediacy that did not disguise or discriminate against social class and background. This tension between a street, or popular, culture and a high culture coalesced during the 1930s when the quintessential subject was the so-called common man. The development of both newspaper photography (photojournalism) and the documentary style ensured that, photographed on location, individuals would be represented in context, resulting in a more intimate image. Morgan Smith recalled being invited to social functions with the request "[B]ring your camera," indicating his subjects' collaboration as his social life reinforced his professional opportunities and vice versa (see Fig. 2.1).[14]

Both Smiths continually submitted photographs to the *Amsterdam News* as well as to other leading black papers, earning, Morgan Smith recalled, $1.50 per picture sold. The sale of their photographs provided the Smiths with an important source of supplemental income during the lean years of the depression.

New York and the Black Press

New York, a vital center for the American press, was also the birthplace of several crusading black papers, including Frederick Douglass's *North Star*, later *Frederick Douglass's Paper* (1845–1860); Marcus Garvey's *Negro World* (1920s), and T. Thomas Fortune's *New York Age* (1880s–1940s). In the early 1930s the *Age*, politically Republican, was the most prominent paper in Harlem. However, the *Amsterdam News*, founded in 1909, soon overtook the *Age* to become Harlem's leading paper.

To be successful, the *Amsterdam News* had to carve a new territory. Rather than cover national issues, the paper's founder, James Anderson, focused on local news and gossip as well as the paper's extensive society section. Under publisher Sadie Warren Davis (1926–1935), the paper expanded, adding a features section, sports section, guest opinion pages, and a high percentage of advertising. The *Amsterdam News* replicated the *Age*'s broadsheet format but followed a tabloid reportage style.

This mixture of genres and the paper's Democratic leanings were contributing factors to the *Amsterdam News*'s rise, and the paper soon all but eclipsed the Age.[15] Indeed, the growth and development of the black press during the 1930s was widely reported on by writers working for the Federal Writers' Project. In the words of one FWP writer, the black papers added "diversified departments of human interest" while taking "many steps forward in the skillful handling of its news, features and pictorial design." The writer goes on to note that "many papers acquire a staff photographer and take great pains to secure the latest and most exclusive pictures"(Fig. 2.6).[16]

Although the *Amsterdam News* rose in popularity, throughout the 1930s the paper was the site of bitter disputes between the publishers and the editorial staff. In a period that saw the dramatic dissolution of the economic system, the depression generation began to challenge what was relevant in news coverage. The demand for a new definition of purpose that went beyond "respectability"—beyond a focus on individual achievement rather than an analysis based on complex sociopolitical factors—became the key conflict between the editors and publishers. The editorial battles waged were influenced by the economic crisis. Addressing issues such as poverty, work, relief, and hiring practices in Harlem—in short, the social issues left in the aftermath of the depression—took on a moral dimension that characterized the editorial content during entire period. The young editorial staff, eager to break into the major media "downtown," agitated for professional recognition to make the paper reflect these contemporary issues.

After a prolonged strike by the editorial staff, the paper was sold in 1936 to Drs. C. B. Powell and P. M. H. Savory, leading Harlem doctors and insurance businessmen.[17] For several months after Powell and Savory took over the paper, the young editors received carte blanche in creating a more modern paper. Utilizing graphic arts, including cartoons (by the emerging talents Oliver Harrington and Bill Chase), the *Amsterdam News* also sought photographs that depicted Harlem not as impoverished but as socially active, both in politics and in entertainment (Figs. 2.8–2.14).

The *Amsterdam News* continued to cultivate readership by appealing to an intellectual and educated audience while at the same time seeking a mass audience through its reliance on sensational stories. The *People's Voice*, the *Amsterdam News*'s chief competitor in Harlem from 1942 to 1948, sought the same audience but looked to broaden its base among the rank-and-file workers in the Harlem community. The key distinction between the two was in their mission: the *Amsterdam News* was run as a business with an eye to profit, whereas the *People's Voice* was a crusading journal, furthering particular political causes and careers, and inspiring its readership to political action.

Morgan Smith and the Amsterdam News

Morgan Smith recalls how he began his career as a photojournalist.

> I would either read about [an event] in the papers or get announcements about what was going on. The person's name was the thing that attracted me. Then I would try to release [the photograph] to the papers. I remember that there were black judges and other people that would be at some event or something like that, and they would appear there. And I would take the pictures of the signing, or the dedication, or opening. Now there was no newsworthiness in something like that for the white press . . . so I sent it out to the black press . . . without assignment . . . or being paid for it.[18]

Smith's statement suggests how he established a market for the documentation of events he independently photographed. Although the papers did not initially provide a budget for a staff photographer, Smith's acumen on what was news and what was casual photography continued to expand during the mid 1930s. Morgan Smith became so adept at on-the-scene photography that he managed to be one of the first photographers on the scene at Penn Station when the first of the "Scottsboro boys" was set free (Fig. 2.15). Since Harlem was the site of so many social and political activities, the Smiths were able to chronicle organized efforts by established protest organizations. For example, the Smiths' photographs of the different demonstrations arising out of the NAACP's antilynching campaign enabled the press to keep this issue visible to an audience removed from, but quite familiar with, living conditions in the South (Fig. 2.16). The photographs blend frozen action and visual information on par with mainstream newspaper photography of that period.

Even the *Amsterdam News*'s new publishers could not altogether ignore Smith's photographs of organized labor, in particular the "Don't Buy Where You Can't Work" campaign, in which the popular pastor Adam Clayton Powell Jr. first came to the public eye, and the grassroots movements that, in many cases, stemmed from Harlem's street corner orators (Figs. 2.17 and 2.18). In the latter photograph, taken from above and notable for its energized movement, Morgan Smith captures the rhythm, energy, and excitement of the urban street—crowded and in flux. The crowd appears to swirl around the orator, whose impassioned look holds the center of the frame. To the right, a train moves off frame, blurring the edge.

In 1937 Morgan Smith entered the *New York Herald-Tribune* amateur photography contest, in which his photograph of a young boy playing "hi-li," a game that was a big summer craze, won first prize

(Fig. 2.19). This photograph contains the freezing of action in an urban setting as a young boy is caught up in his ball game. The publicity surrounding the contest brought Morgan to the attention of the Powell and Savory Corporation. Hired as the *Amsterdam News*'s first staff photographer toward the end of 1937, Morgan Smith and the paper's editors (notably Obie McCullum and Roi Ottley) sought to diversify news coverage with the introduction of photo-essays. For several months the paper ran Morgan's essays on topics ranging from opening night at Harlem's Lafayette Theater to an intimate portrayal of boxing great Joe Louis at the rise of his career.

Morgan Smith and Joe Louis

Smith's photographs of Joe Louis for the *Amsterdam News* represent a significant body of work. During the 1930s Louis emerged from the margin to the center as a new type of "race" leader, a sports star, a powerful symbol in the mass media. Louis was widely written about—indeed, he captured the imagination of the generation.[19] Writers such as James Weldon Johnson and Richard Wright defined the impact of Louis, who, through his fists and against white opponents, fought his way to the top. Wright put it succinctly: "Joe was the consecrated essence of black triumph over white."[20] The *Amsterdam News* understood that Louis's symbolic importance placed him, in the national consciousness, well ahead of past heroes such as Frederick Douglass, Booker T. Washington, and Marcus Garvey. Louis came to symbolize not just a sport, but the struggle against racism. He appealed to a mass audience of African Americans and other sympathetic groups on a scale never before achieved. Unlike his predecessors in "race" leadership, Louis had the mass media establishment covering his actions; he was photographed continually from 1935 through the war years. The coverage of Louis went beyond boxing and sports, lending racial issues a national focus.

Morgan Smith's photographs of Louis for the *Amsterdam News* are unique for their intimacy. The Smiths and Louis became friends during this period, and the relationship allowed Morgan to portray Louis in his more personal moments. Initially, however, the Smiths were accorded less access than the mainstream photographers. Smith's first coverage in 1936, therefore, focused primarily on Louis's wife, Marva, who apparently was more accessible and less in demand by the mass media while also of great interest to an African American audience. Through the coverage of Marva, Smith helped to cultivate Louis's image as a "devoted family man," although it was rumored he had many extra-marital affairs (Fig. 2.20).[21]

Throughout Louis's career, the black press cast Marva as the foil whenever he failed to live up to his orchestrated public representation. For example, when Louis suffered his greatest defeat in 1936 by the German boxer Max Schmeling, syndicated articles appearing in the *Amsterdam News* blamed Marva. In articles that proliferated throughout the black press, it was rumored that Marva argued with her husband before the fight. Further articles alleged Marva paid off a former boyfriend so that she would be free to marry Louis. Clearly, less was at stake in attacking Marva. To criticize her behavior would not be interpreted as undermining the efforts of Louis.

In examining the photographs by the Smiths, one sees why Marva may have fallen victim to such scapegoating. Unlike the somewhat camera-shy Louis, Marva appeared to enjoy the attention she received. The Smiths captured Marva Louis as sexy and playful. These portraits of Marva foreshadow the brothers' later portrait-studio work, in which aspiring models become their most creative clientele. The Smiths' photographs of Marva are among the earliest collaborative explorations between photographer and model in which both beauty and personality adorn the portrait. In their portraits of women in particular, sensuality becomes an added dimension. The Smiths' coy portrayal of Marva, combined with the *Amsterdam News*'s enthusiastic coverage of her—which included numerous articles on her clothes, her charm, and her appearances throughout New York black society— changed after Louis was defeated by Schmeling in 1936. Marva, now dismissed as frivolous, all but disappeared from the *Amsterdam News* in the months that followed Louis's defeat.

For Morgan Smith, however, Louis's defeat proved a professional boon. Smith was now regularly assigned to Louis during his training. His early assignments depict the boxer as chagrined but hardworking. The *Amsterdam News* utilized many of Smith's photographs in photo-essays and full-page collages. One layout from August 15, 1936, is a notable example. The caption states that Louis is "through with loafing," insidiously reaffirming a racist ideology of African Americans in general and indicating the doubt the press had about Louis and his ability to be a "race" leader. Smith's coverage, however, photographically redeems Louis. Pictured in close-ups during training, Louis appears single-minded, even when he is visited by prominent individuals and the press (Fig. 2.21). Louis always maintained his composure and determination. Ultimately, Smith's photographs and the editorial collage served to blunt the criticism aimed at the boxer.

Overall, Smith's approach to Louis followed the formal, full-frame snapshot popular in news overage. Smith did not get his subject to collaborate on a more dramatic vision, as he did with Marva and as he would later do with Adam Clayton Powell Jr. Indeed, judging by the photographic evidence, Louis never seemed to enjoy the public glare, or at least did not appear to revel in it. Through the Smiths' coverage in the *Amsterdam News* and the mass media, Louis became a powerful symbol of achievement, occupying a position above the racist court of public opinion. When Louis won a fight, large crowds would gather to celebrate throughout Harlem. His victories served as an example of what might be possible in the United States in the 1930s.

Editorial Conflict at the *Amsterdam News*

During 1936 and 1937 the editorial staff at the *Amsterdam News* found the new owners less sympathetic to adopting changes in the paper than the staff had hoped. The editors were never able to fully implement the new columns and departments they sought in order to diversify the paper. The new publishers adhered to (in the words of one of their reporters) "the dictates of society, not making any impression at all, not addressing the problems that faced people in [Harlem]."[22] Politically progressive articles concerning labor and workplace were relegated to the inside pages. Pressure to leave out these issues in assigning stories was noted during a grievance hearing in 1936.[23] These conflicts illustrated the dilemma between what sold newspapers (society coverage and sensational stories) and what had direct relevance to the lives of most of the readers.

Creative editors such as T. R. Poston and writer Henry Lee Moon tried to add features such as an investigative series on crime, an in-depth analysis that tied crime into social conditions instead of the sensational aspects of crime itself. These men and others on the staff strove to make the paper relevant to the issues of the period. Politically, the editorial staff was aided by the progressive climate in New York, known as the "popular front," in which left-wing groups worked together during the economic crisis to support the New Deal.[24] Whenever possible, they would assign stories on labor and social issues. But the secondary treatment these stories were ultimately accorded made the paper unpopular among political activists in Harlem.

The ideological battle between commerce and social responsibility led to a fractious relationship between owners and staff. Although the new publishers gave little thought to expanding the budget for photographs, they recognized, as did the editors, that photographs enhanced the appearance of the paper. To the editorial staff, expanding the cartoons and photography served an additional function. As Oliver Harrington, the art director at the *People's Choice*, noted, "[T]he editorial cartoon was extremely necessary in newspapers, especially where people were rushing into the subway to go to work and [did] the same thing to come home at night. And cartoons would supply much more information and ideas and feelings than anything else in the newspaper . . . and the same is true for photographs."[25] Photography and cartoons became the site wherein social and political issues would not only be given visibility but would be easily understood. Nevertheless, the photographers, who were also considered editorial staff, felt the sting of bitter working conditions at the *Amsterdam News*. As Morgan Smith recalled:

[The *Amsterdam News*] supplied nothing . . . no equipment, no material, and no transportation. . . . And they got to the point where they wanted to pay me per photograph [rather than salary], which was a dollar and a half per picture. And you spend [your own] money and run all over Brooklyn and take the picture and bring it back. And then you got the picture and they'd select maybe two or three out of a dozen . . . but the thing that sort of saved me was that I began to syndicate pictures to other publications. Because I wasn't getting enough from [the *Amsterdam News*]. They wanted exclusive rights to all the pictures at that time, but I wouldn't give it.[26]

Faced with limited options, Smith endured these difficult working conditions. He recognized the significance of maintaining control over his work in order to do business with competing black papers, keeping all of his options, however limited, open.

A Paper for the People: The Formation of the *People's Voice*

As a young man, Adam Clayton Powell Jr., then a pastor at the Abyssinian Baptist Church in Harlem, participated in street demonstrations against unfair hiring practices and discrimination in Harlem. He recognized the political opportunity someone of his stature could claim both among the working people of Harlem and among Harlem society. In the early 1930s, Powell was invited to write a column for the *Amsterdam News*. His "Soap Box" column became a permanent fixture in the paper and gave him a broad audience for his political views. Powell offers an interesting counterpoint to Joe Louis. Both men were widely covered by the black press. But while Louis's position as a "race" leader was cast in symbolic terms, Powell sought definition as a defiant, unequivocal leader. The "politics of respectability," an ideology crucial to an earlier period, still informed the editorial discourse while undergoing a transformation under the vastly different landscape of the depression and early war effort. Now respectability was recast in terms of political progressivism and political representation. But the *Amsterdam News* failed to keep up with the transformation. There was indeed a vacuum in New York that could be filled by a crusading paper that would align itself with the political and progressive aims and address daily injustices. As one *Amsterdam News* reader put it: "Why doesn't your paper print some real news? [N]ews that will be something to help the Negro, not news to bring our race down. If you want something to publish, why don't you publish about our economic conditions, our housing conditions, our crooked politicians, preachers and other crooked rackets in Harlem?"[27]

In 1942, Adam Clayton Powell, assessing the political landscape that had brought him election to the city council—a victory that had shocked an older generation of black leaders as well as the New York City political machine known as Tammany Hall—began to accumulate political power, both within the Harlem community and in New York City, and began his own newspaper, the *People's Voice*.[28] The newspaper was backed financially by Savoy Ballroom owner and copublisher Charles Buchanan, and the first issue appeared on February 14, 1942, after Powell's first month on the council.

The war years proved to hold more opportunities for black newspapers, as major companies received tax credits on their advertising budgets.[29] This, and Powell's own position, made it viable to leave out the offensive racial advertising. The editorial focus of the paper echoed Powell's political platform: "better housing, an end to racial discrimination in all forms, better schools, full job opportunities in the private sector, support for Negro Businesses." Major coverage was devoted to Powell and his ascending political career (Fig. 2.22).[30]

Borrowing from the familiar trope of individual achievement (an "uplift" strategy), Adam Clayton Powell sought to publish a socially relevant paper. He did so by changing his emphasis to a more working-class-oriented concept. Using the language of militancy, Powell sought to fill the charismatic leadership position left vacant for over a decade following the deportation of Marcus Garvey in December 1927. Unlike Garvey, however, Powell worked inside the structure of mainstream politics.

The *People's Voice* adopted a tabloid format, which allowed for bigger photographs and an overall better design. Several important influences went into its shaping. One was St. Clair Bourne, the paper's first managing editor. Bourne, with Powell's approval, formulated how the news was to be presented and the layout of the paper, and assigned photographic coverage. Bourne remembers that

Smith was the preferred photographer among the editors. Not only did he get good images, he could also be sent without a reporter and bring back enough information to write up a photo caption, something other photographers would not necessarily undertake. In 1943, after Bourne left the paper, Powell hired Marvel Cooke, who later became the paper's assistant managing editor.[31] Cooke had been at the *Amsterdam News*, where she was one of the first female reporters in the news division. At the *People's Voice*, Cooke's role shifted to copy editing and makeup and then to working directly at the printing plant each week. These skills she had learned fifteen years earlier while working under W. E. B. Du Bois at the journal *Crisis*. According to Cooke, layout and editorial decisions were made in weekly meetings attended by Powell. She recalled Powell's penchant for sensational headlines, although the paper took a different tack from that of its main competitors at the *Amsterdam News*. Instead of murder and other types of crime, the *People's Voice* worked to expose political corruption and bias in federal and city government.

Another staff member whose opinion held considerable sway with Powell was the general manager, Doxey Wilkerson, who had been a prominent professor at Howard University. According to Cooke, Wilkerson's job was to ensure that the copy reflected Powell's political platform and also incorporated Wilkerson's labor-oriented position. (Wilkerson was also a member of the Communist Party, as were several other key staff members, a crucial element in the paper's demise in 1948, when it became an early victim of the McCarthy era.)[32]

Cooke also remarks that former New York City Councilman Ben Davis, at that time a political protégé of Powell's, served as the "editorial department behind the editorial department."[33] She credits Davis for keeping Powell politically informed and focused, and for the paper's role in building a readership among a community of working-class people, not only the bourgeoisie. Davis, the former editor of the Communist paper the *Negro Liberator* and a columnist at the *New York Daily World*, also made suggestions for what stories would run in the paper.

Cooke was a fervent supporter of the *People's Voice* and saw it as separate from Powell and his political aspirations. She believed that "there was a desperate need for a paper which would help build the community rather than sensationalize it."[34] Oral testimonies from Cooke, Bourne, and art director Oliver Harrington attest to the diverse issues and decisions they faced in putting the paper together. Ultimately, however, the paper was Powell's and he had final say on everything, including the photographs.[35]

Adam Powell and Morgan Smith: The Construction of Power

Powell created the term "Marching Black" to identify the political movement promoted by him and the *People's Voice*. Powell also used the term self-referentially to crystallize the image that he was creating for himself. In discussing Powell and the *People's Voice*, it is important to examine what this term symbolized socially, and how it was distinct from traditional representation.

For Powell the term "Marching Black" suggested a tradition of revolution beginning with the founding of the United States. He posited African Americans as the inheritors of this revolutionary tradition, but he reshaped the issues to reflect the concerns of the war years. The language of Powell's "Soap Box" columns reflected an active voice, underscoring a political urgency. He staked his claim to leadership with his pronouncement, "My father said that he built the church, but I would interpret it. This I made up my mind to do."[36] Powell, then, was clear in his intention to control his own interpretation. His adoption of "Black" signaled a break with the more popular "Negro." "Black" struck a chord of militancy, especially when juxtaposed with "Marching." If this was how Powell's paper differentiated itself from its competitors, it also pointed the differences out to a white audience who saw the black press as one mass organ. Seeking to participate in Powell's campaign, Morgan Smith cultivated and developed a new form of photographic coverage that led to a new mode of representation in the newspaper.

Morgan Smith began working for the *People's Voice* soon after the first issue was released. He covered the February 21, 1942, "Social Event of the Week," the thirty-third birthday ball for the NAACP. The photo credit lists Smith as the staff photographer, although he was, at this time, in the midst of running his own studio with his brother.[37] The photographic style of the story was not dissimilar from the approach Smith used at the *Amsterdam News*. However, the assignments Smith received for the *People's Voice* soon began to affect his approach, as he turned away from social events and instead focused on other issues the paper sought to spotlight.

As a photographer, Smith matured while working for the *People's Voice*. His pictures took on a looser, more experimental quality. One factor contributing to this may have been his use of the flash attachment to the Speed Graphic camera. Another factor in Smith's maturation was his visual development through the operation of his own commercial studio. By 1942 Smith had operated his studio full-time for three years and had learned about lighting, sets, and makeup. It was no longer enough to simply, or candidly, snap the photograph; there was now an element of theater in his practice.

Perhaps the most dynamic series of pictures by Smith were done for the crime section. While Marvel Cooke maintains that the *People's Voice* aimed to get away from scandal reporting, Smith's photographs offer an interesting contradiction. These photographs can also be seen as influencing his approach to other subjects. As Cooke notes, crime and scandal added little political or social value to the paper's editorial objectives. Nonetheless, the crime images belong to what art historian Jane Livingston terms the "New York School." Livingston defines this approach as a mode of capturing the life of the city that reflects both its fluidity and its social structure. Smith's crime photographs belong to that aesthetic because of the distinctly urban subject matter and his use of the Speed Graphic camera, an important tool in the development of the style.[38] A great example is a photograph in the May 30, 1942, issue. Smith photographed Harlem street gamblers from a rooftop, capturing them unaware (Fig. 2.23). This picture represents a breakthrough for Smith. The high angle emphasizes a sense of the "underworld." (In film at this time Orson Welles employed such oblique angles to represent psychological states; they were also a way to visually elucidate a social criticism.)

In subsequent issues, Smith treated several subjects in a similar manner: a war parade, Madame Chiang Kai-shek, and, finally, Powell at a street rally (Fig. 2.24). This new rendering of Powell emphasizes leadership through his position of dominance in the frame. Housed in the Prints and Photographs Division at the Schomburg Center for Research in Black Culture is the original contact sheet from this series. With it one can trace Smith's innovative approach to documenting Powell. Not content to position himself at level with the subject, Smith utilized neighboring buildings above and across from where Powell was speaking. The photographer took on a different role in relation to his subject. In a sense, Smith gave his photographs the editorial focus that was lacking in his earlier work. His photographs could no longer be read as neutral or straight reportage. They represent a self-conscious attempt to stylize and invest the subject with an aura of power.

Conclusion

A dynamic reading of Smith's photographs linking the newspapers to his photographs reflects both a personal vision and popular style. This is an era that was marked by a social and political transition within the black intelligentsia. While most of the prominent figures of the teens and twenties still occupied positions of influence, a younger generation had begun to emerge. Change was evident in the political demonstrations and programs that addressed the social and economic imbalance for African Americans. This new militancy was first seen in the embrace of Joe Louis and later captured by Adam Powell.[39] The new leaders sought to define themselves as distinct from their predecessors. Like other political leaders, they increasingly found that the most effective way to promote an agenda was through the network of the mass media, including the expansive network of the black press.

Belonging to both the tradition of racial uplift and the emerging civil rights movement—or Marching Blacks—Smith's work negotiates between these two oftentimes opposing strategies. The theory of racial uplift saw the struggle for social equality as essentially a self-help project (accommodating the dominant society), whereas the civil rights movement moved into an activist, interventionist strategy (challenging the dominant society). Of course, these ideas are far more complex than this simple reductive explanation, but it was the merging of these two extremes that characterized the political discourse of the major periodicals of the black press during the 1930s. Each paper Smith worked for seemed to occupy an opposing place on that spectrum. The *Amsterdam News* adhered to popular culture in its coverage of social and political issues, but always reflected the theory of racial uplift; and the *People's Voice* promoted a progressive political ideology. Within this contested terrain of representation and identity, Smith cultivated a sophisticated journalistic practice that visually articulated crucial issues facing the United States during the 1930s and the war years.

Notes

This paper was researched and written under the auspices of the 1994 Scholar-in-Residency program at Schomburg Center for Research in Black Culture, New York, and funded by the National Endowment on the Humanities.

1. During the Roosevelt years, the Farm Security Administration, the Federal Arts Projects, and the National Youth Administration all had photographic projects attached to them. Additionally, photojournalism, exemplified by *Life* magazine (1936), is included in this time period.

2. "It was during this period that we find, for the first time, frequent references to an 'American Way of Life.' The phrase 'The American Dream' came into common use." Warren I. Susman, "The Thirties," in *The Development of an American Culture*, 2d rev. ed., ed. Stanley Coben and Lorman Ratner (New York: St. Martin's Press, 1983), p. 221.

3. See William Stott, *Documentary Expression and Thirties America* (New York: Oxford University Press, 1973).

4. See especially Maricia Battle, *Harlem Photographs, 1932–1940, by Aaron Siskind* (New Haven, Conn.: Eastern Press and the Smithsonian Institution Press, 1990); Henry Louis Gates, "The Trope of the New Negro," *Representations* 24 (fall 1988); Nicholas Natanson, *The Black Image in the New Deal: The Politics of FSA Photography* (Knoxville: University of Tennessee Press, 1992); Sally Stein, "Figures of the Future: Photography of the National Youth Administration," in *Official Images: New Deal Photography*, ed. Pete Daniel and Sally Stein (Washington, D.C.: Smithsonian Institution Press,

1987), pp. 92–147; Deborah Willis, *James VanDerZee* (New York: Abrams, 1994).

5. Angela Davis, "Photography and Afro-American History," Ten 8 (24): p. 5.

6. Author's interviews with former editors: St. Clair Bourne, May 3, 1994; Marvel Cooke, March 31, 1994; Oliver Harrington, February 17, 1994; and photographer Austin Hansen, June 8, 1994.

7. See the Marvin and Morgan Smith Portfolio Collection in the Department of Prints and Photographs, Schomburg Center for Research in Black Culture, New York Public Library.

8. Morgan Smith, interview with the author, June 5, 1992.

9. Larry A. Greene, "Harlem in the Great Depression" (Ph.D. diss., Columbia University, 1979), p. iii.

10. Sculptor Augusta Savage had returned to New York from Europe by the 1930s, settling in Harlem. Savage opened her studio for free workshops and informal study for residents in her Harlem neighborhood, which was rapidly becoming a center for artistic activity. With the formation of the Federal Arts Project in 1935–36, Savage was given funding and opened as the Harlem Art Center. Savage structured the classes as informal studio sessions. Neither Smith recalls being told how to draw or paint; rather it was the atmosphere of the artists' community that became the center's most lasting legacy. Such now well-known artists as Aaron Douglas, Jacob Lawrence, Gwendolyn Knight, Robert Blackburn, Elba Lightfoot, E. Simms Campbell, and Charles Alston were among the Smiths' newfound community. For a detailed analysis of the Harlem Art Center, Savage, and the Federal Arts Project in Harlem, see Kim Carlton Smith, "A New Deal for Women: Women Artists and the Federal Arts Project, 1935–1939" (Ph.D. diss., Rutgers University, 1990).

11. E. Franklin Frazier, *Black Bourgeoisie* (Glencoe, Ill.: Free Press, 1957). Frazier actually uses this term as a critique of the materialism and conspicuous consumption of the black middle class.

12. Smith interview.

13. In studying design manuals from the first half of this century, one notes the common use of illustrative framing in newspaper design. Additionally, *New York Amsterdam News* society portraits, many taken by Harlem photographer James Latimer Allen, are notable for the incorporation of the added framing. See also R. Randolph Karch, *Basic Lesson in Printing Layout* (Milwaukee, Wis.: Bruce Publishing, 1952), p. 32.

14. Smith interview. The *Amsterdam News* retained the advertising broker W. B. Ziff, head of an advertising agency of the same name. Ziff, who was white, was accused of holding "a commercial stranglehold on the Negro press." During a labor dispute at the paper, the editorial staff questioned his role and involvement at the paper as a broker and as a business manager. Particularly offensive was that his entire business was based upon promoting "racial" products that reaffirmed an Anglo-American appearance. Ziff's company received a 45 percent commission for these ads. This fee was considered exorbitant by the editorial staff at the *Amsterdam News*, who attacked Ziff during the labor dispute of 1936. Judge James Watson Papers, *Amsterdam News* file, Manuscripts, Archives, and Rare Books Division, Schomburg Center for Research in Black Culture. For further information, see Vishnu V. Oak, *The Negro Newspaper* (Yellowsprings, Ohio: Antioch Press, 1948), p. 133.

15. A 1949 independent report lists the circulation of the *Amsterdam News* at the high figure of 105,322, while the *People's Voice* (founded in 1942 and discussed later) is listed at 16,388, a typical figure for those years. Richard Robbins, "Counter-Assertion in the New York Negro Press," *Phylon* (Atlanta University), no. 2 (1949): p. 126.

16. Snelson, "Negro Press: Contributions in Make Up" (1936 entry), in *Negroes of New York: Forty-three Studies of the History of Black People in the City of New York* (New York: Works Progress Administration, 1936–1941), in Manuscripts, Archives, and Rare Books Division, Schomburg Center for Research in Black Culture.

17. The 1935 editorial strike at the *Amsterdam News* galvanized the Harlem community, with all the major black papers

and several white papers covering the three-month conflict. At issue was not so much wages but creative control. A vivid oral history of the strike is found in Marvel Cooke, "The Reminiscences of Marvel Cooke," *Women in Journalism Oral History Project* (New York: Washington Press Club Foundation, Columbia University Oral History Research Office, 1991).

18. Smith interview.

19. A thorough discussion of Louis's impact on intellectuals can be found in Gerald Early, "The Black Intellectual and the Sport of Prizefighting," in *The Culture of Bruising: Essays on Prizefighting, Literature, and Modern American Culture*, ed. Gerald Early (Hopewell, N.J.: Ecco Press, 1994), pp. 5–45. Also see Jeffrey T. Sammons, *Beyond the Ring: The Role of Boxing in American Society* (Urbana: University of Illinois Press, 1988).

20. Richard Wright, "Joe Louis Uncovers Dynamite," *New York Daily World*, October 8, 1935.

21. In this, Louis parallels Powell, a known "ladies' man." However, Powell never hid this from the public. Instead he constructed the playboy image as glamorous, not shameful. See Chris Mead, *Champion: Joe Louis, Black Hero in White America* (New York: Scribner, 1985). Mead notes that reporters in the thirties routinely left out potentially damaging information. "As an indication of the journalistic custom of looking the other way, sports writers never made an issue of the backgrounds of Roxborough, Black, or Blackburn, although they knew that Louis's managers were numbers men and that Blackburn had served time for manslaughter" (p. 54).

22. Cooke, "The Reminiscences of Marvel Cooke," p. 66.

23. See Judge James S. Watson Papers, Schomburg Center for Research in Black Culture, *Amsterdam News* file, "Hearing before James S. Watson," May 18, 1930.

24. See Cheryl Lynn Greenberg, *"Or Does It Explode?" Black Harlem in the Great Depression* (New York: Oxford University Press, 1991); Mark Naison, *Communists in Harlem during the Depression* (Urbana: University of Illinois Press, 1983); Dominic J. Capeci Jr., *The Harlem Riot of 1943* (Philadelphia: Temple University Press, 1977); Greene, *Harlem in the Great Depression*.

25. Harrington interview.

26. Smith interview.

27. F. Parker, "Views on Many Questions," *New York Amsterdam News*, July 29, 1939.

28. A. Phillip Randolph was reportedly being groomed for this newly districted office. Powell's ultimate inclusion on the ballot represented something of a political coup. See Herbert Bruce Papers (1930–1960), Manuscripts, Archives, and Rare Books Division, Schomburg Center for Research in Black Culture.

29. Mary Alice Sentman and Patrick S. Washburn, "How Excess Profits Tax Brought Ads to Black Newspapers in World War II," *Journalism Quarterly* (University of Southern Carolina) 65 (winter 1988): pp. 764–44.

30. Charles V. Hamilton, *Adam Clayton Powell Jr.: The Political Biography of an American Dilemma* (New York: Atheneum, 1991), p. 119. Much confusion exists about the relationship of the *People's Voice* to an innovative picture newspaper, *PM Daily*, edited by Ralph Ingersoll and published by the Chicago clothier Marshall Field. To date, I have not found enough information to unravel the connection. However, Oliver Harrington remembers that the *People's Voice* used the same printing plant and this association led to speculation that Marshall Field, who was white, was behind the *People's Voice*. These rumors persisted throughout the paper's history, calling into question Powell's designation of the paper as part of the black press and other issues regarding the paper's financing. Marvel Cooke alludes to inauspicious funding coming through connections Buchanan had at the Savoy Ballroom, but she does not clarify her meaning. Actually, the paper was plagued by financial troubles throughout its six-year history. See also an article appearing in *Time*, June 15, 1942, which

alleges Marshall Field donated twenty-five thousand dollars to the *People's Voice; People's Voice*, June 20, 1942; Adam Clayton Powell, "The Politics of PV," and Marvel Cooke, "PV and the Community," both in *People's Voice*, February 17, 1945; and Roy Hoopes, *Ralph Ingersoll: A Biography* (New York: Atheneum, 1985), p. 216.

31. Bourne interview. According to Cooke, Powell never promoted her because he was uncomfortable with a woman running the paper, indicative of his sexist attitude toward women, an attitude common during that period. Cooke interview.

32. Cooke interview.

33. Cooke, "The Reminiscences of Marvel Cooke," p. 92.

34. Ibid.

35. Cooke interview; Cooke, "The Reminiscences of Marvel Cooke"; Bourne interview; Harrington interview.

36. Adam Clayton Powell, *Marching Blacks* (New York: Dell Press, 1945), p. 94.

37. Smith placed advertisements for his studio in the paper on a regular basis throughout 1942.

38. Smith also remembers meeting Weegee, New York's most infamous crime photographer, who worked for the *Daily News*, while out shooting for the newspapers. Weegee's now legendary coverage of New York crime may have had an influence on Smith's approach.

39. My focus here is on male leadership. See recent studies conducted by Patricia Hill Collins, Evelyn Brooks Higginbotham, and Darlene Clark Hines on the crucial leadership role of African American women.

2.1 Lucien Aigner, *Morgan and Marvin Smith*, late 1930s. © Lucien Aigner Studio.

2.2 Morgan and Marvin Smith, *Augusta Savage*, 1937. The Smiths studied with Savage, a renowned sculptor and educator, when they first arrived in Harlem in 1933. In 1937, Savage was commissioned to make *Lift Every Voice and Sing* (pictured here), a sculpture for the New York World's Fair, and she did not return to teaching. Schomburg Center for Research in Black Culture, New York Public Library.

2.3 Morgan and Marvin Smith, *Langston Hughes*, ca. 1940. A leading poet and writer during and after the Harlem Renaissance, Langston Hughes was often a prominent figure in the society and news sections of the *Amsterdam News*. This photograph for the newspaper was taken at Hughes's home at 141st Street and St. Nicholas Avenue. Schomburg Center for Research in Black Culture, New York Public Library.

2.4 Morgan and Marvin Smith, *Portrait of Duke Ellington*, 1943. Schomburg Center for Research in Black Culture, New York Public Library.

2.5 Morgan and Marvin Smith, *Ella Fitzgerald,* ca. 1938. Here she performs with the Chick Webb Orchestra at the Savoy Ballroom; Louis Jordan is seated to her left. The Smiths were self-proclaimed "stage-door Johnnies" and often sought out entertainers and performers with the objective of taking their photographs. Schomburg Center for Research in Black Culture, New York Public Library.

2.6 Morgan and Marvin Smith, *Mr. and Mrs. Jesse Owens*, 1936. This photograph was taken upon the Owens' arrival in New York after the 1936 Olympics. Schomburg Center for Research in Black Culture, New York Public Library.

2.7 Morgan and Marvin Smith, *Mrs. Noble Sissle, Hyacinth Curtis, and Actress Fredi Washington*, ca. 1944. Fredi Washington is perhaps best known for the 1934 Hollywood film *Imitation of Life*. She was quite active in social and political causes in Harlem. Washington consistently refused the stereotypical roles offered to African American women and, as a result, went for long periods with no work. In 1935 Washington's sister, Isabel, married Adam Clayton Powell Jr. When Powell began his newspaper, the *People's Voice*, in 1942, Fredi began writing a popular weekly column that investigated hiring and other unfair practices in the acting field. Schomburg Center for Research in Black Culture, New York Public Library.

2.8 Morgan and Marvin Smith, *Easter Sunday in Harlem*, 1939. Schomburg Center for Research in Black Culture, New York Public Library.

2.9 Morgan and Marvin Smith, *Transit Workers Union Strike*, 1940. Schomburg Center for Research in Black Culture, New York Public Library.

2.10 Morgan and Marvin Smith, *Curley, Lionel, and Red Hampton at the Apollo*, 1942. Schomburg Center for Research in Black Culture, New York Public Library.

2.11 Morgan and Marvin Smith, *Paul Robeson Gives Autograph to Reul Lester after Robeson's Concert at the Mother A.M.E. Zion Church in Harlem*, 1940. Schomburg Center for Research in Black Culture, New York Public Library.

2.12 Morgan and Marvin Smith, *Katherine Dunham and an Unidentified Dancer in Performance at the Apollo,* 1942. Schomburg Center for Research in Black Culture, New York Public Library.

2.13 Morgan and Marvin Smith, *Richmond Barthé with Bust of Abraham Lincoln*, n.d. Schomburg Center for Research in Black Culture, New York Public Library.

2.14 Morgan and Marvin Smith, *Savoy Ballroom Lindy Hoppers,* 1938. They include, *second from left*, Thomas "Tops" Lee; on the bandstand, Charles Buchanan; and, *in the foreground*, Tiny Bunch. Schomburg Center for Research in Black Culture, New York Public Library.

2.15 Morgan and Marvin Smith, *Scottsboro Boys Arrive in New York, Penn Station*, July 1937. *Left to right*: Roy Wright, Olen Montgomery, attorney Samuel Leibowitz, and Willie Robinson. Dominating the news in both the black and mainstream press during the 1930s was the case known as Scottsboro. In 1931 nine young men, ages thirteen to twenty, were arrested for hoboing near Scottsboro, Alabama. Also arrested on the same freight car were two white women who later alleged they were raped. Although these allegations were false, all nine were arrested, convicted of rape, and sentenced to death. The NAACP and the American Communist Party fought for the release of the "Scottsboro boys" for almost ten years. These three young men were the first of the nine to be released from prison. Schomburg Center for Research in Black Culture, New York Public Library.

2.16 Morgan and Marvin Smith, *Antilynching Demonstration*, 1937. In 1933 the NAACP prepared a first draft of an antilynching bill with Colorado senator Edward Costigan and New York senator Robert Wagner as its cosponsors. The bill remained in filibuster, led by southern and conservative senators, for many years. Although the bill was never passed and was eventually dropped in 1942, the campaign brought great visibility to the issue and invigorated activists across the country. As part of the NAACP's strategy to keep the issue in the press, groups formed in support of the bill and would demonstrate before or during public events such as the one captured in this photograph.

The original caption read: "Friends of a Federal anti-lynching bill stage a mass picket demonstration Saturday in front of the Strand Theater in Times Square. (The occasion was the release of the Hollywood film *They Won't Forget*.)" Schomburg Center for Research in Black Culture, New York Public Library.

2.17 Morgan and Marvin Smith, *Reverend Adam Clayton Powell Jr., "Don't Buy Where You Can't Work"* *Campaign,* 1942, 125th Street, Harlem. The "Don't Buy Where You Can't Work" campaign begun by street organizer Sufi Abdul Hamid in the 1930s became a leading strategy to make discriminatory hiring practices along Harlem's main shopping district, 125th Street, visible. The large crowds that would gather in support of the demonstrations would virtually block access to the establishment, forcing the owners to respond to the grievance. In this demonstration the workers complained of low wages and lack of vacation time and sick time. Schomburg Center for Research in Black Culture, New York Public Library.

2.18 Morgan and Marvin Smith, *Street Corner Orator,* 1938. Street corner orators, or "soapbox" speakers, were an active part of everyday life in Harlem, especially during the depression. In 1937 the *Amsterdam News* ran an article decrying the then twenty-five-year tradition by claiming: "Harlem will not be saved by them. They are the least of the constructive forces in the community, and while the soap boxer is an institution, soap boxers come and go in the tide of human affairs. Yet he is a necessary evil, and as such, he may be tolerated as the whites tolerate those at Union Square and the English tolerate theirs at Hyde Park." Schomburg Center for Research in Black Culture, New York Public Library.

2.19 Morgan and Marvin Smith, *Boy [Robert Day] Playing Hi-Li*, 1937. Schomburg Center for Research in Black Culture, New York Public Library.

2.20. Morgan and Marvin Smith, *Joe and Marva Louis*, 1938. Schomburg Center for Research in Black Culture, New York Public Library.

2.21 Morgan and Marvin Smith, *Porter Roberts, Joe Louis, St. Clair Bourne, and Billy Rowe*, 1938. Schomburg Center for Research in Black Culture, New York Public Library.

2.22 Morgan and Marvin Smith, *Family of the Week, Staff Members of the* "*People's Voice,*" July 11, 1942. Schomburg Center for Research in Black Culture, New York Public Library.

2.23 Morgan and Marvin Smith, *Dice Game on West 113th Street in Harlem*, 1942. Schomburg Center for Research in Black Culture, New York Public Library.

2.24 Morgan and Marvin Smith, *Reverend Adam Clayton Powell Jr.,* 1942. Powell is shown here chatting with policeman and an unidentified member of the crowd after one of his rallies in Harlem. Schomburg Center for Research in Black Culture, New York Public Library.

3. SEEKING A CULTURAL EQUALITY

THE VISUAL RECORD OF ROBERT H. MCNEILL

Jane Lusaka

Being segregated, you had to live where you were able to live. And there was really a sort of an amalgamation of cultures and educational levels in a given block. They were black people. And they were respected people. . . . You had the iceman who came to the house; you had the people who handled the moving. The lawyers, the teachers; they depended on each other in a sense so that there was a diversity within a neighborhood. No one resented anyone else in particular that you could see because they recognized the social, and the economic, and the educational level of each individual and they came to them for some kind of support and advice.

—Robert H. McNeill
Interview with the author, 1993

Since colonial times, Washington, D.C., has been home to a strong and vibrant African American community. For decades after the Civil War, Washington's black leadership had been in the hands of an "elite group, referred to as the 'Four Hundred of Washington' by Archibald Grimke, [consisting] primarily of political appointees, intellectuals, and a number of ministers and professionals [who were] primarily concerned with restoring the civil and political rights of blacks; they valued above all, the opportunity for full integration."[1] Known as the "cave dwellers," they were also very aware of social status, family pedigree, an--in many cases—their white ancestry, and thought themselves superior to the masses of black people.

But by the turn of the century, Frederick Douglass's message of integration had given way to Booker T. Washington's promise of success through prosperity, as more and more migrants from the South moved into the city. Within the black community, a new class developed that equated "money with high social standing without regard for ancestry, culture or continuity. The new black economic elite, unlike the old upper class, whose occupations brought it into frequent contact with upper-class whites, was tied almost exclusively to the black ghetto and less concerned about assimilation into the larger society."[2]

Pressures came from outside as well as within the community. By the end of World War I, "conditions [had] worsened for District blacks. The screws of segregation were painfully tightened during President Wilson's administration: separate working areas and eating facilities were decreed and the handful of black appointments [established during Reconstruction] were abolished."[3] As one writer notes, "For the first time photographs were required on all civil service applications. The impact [of segregation] was so great that Booker T. Washington could write of an August [1913] visit to the nation's capital: 'I have never seen colored people so discouraged and bitter as they are at the present time.'"[4]

By 1917, the year that photographer Robert H. McNeill was born, Washington had become a divided city, two communities separated by race, each side suspicious and wary of the other. Two years later, the country erupted in turmoil during "Red Summer," when racial and political riots took place in cities throughout the North and South. In Washington, D.C.,

> a mob of white sailors and marines [attacked the black community]. In response to the threat, over 2,000 armed black residents from all over the city, many veterans of the First World War, gathered along U and 7th Streets to defend the neighborhood. [Their] aggressive actions served to defuse and contain the violence of the riots. James Weldon Johnson, the NAACP's traveling secretary, was sent to Washington to investigate the riots. He was impressed, seeing the black response as evidence of a heightened sense of unity and black pride.[5]

Black Washingtonians responded to the new restrictions in several ways, including "protest, public education, and the establishment of organizations fostering civic pride."[6] They began to realize that they had to unite like never before. If they were not wanted in the white world, African Americans would create their own. In this endeavor, photography provided an immediate and accessible tool.

> [T]housands upon thousands of other poor blacks . . . in the first decades of the 20th century, left peasant parents and grandparents and a southern history that was born in chains to come to northern cities—to Detroit, to Chicago, to New York, to Baltimore, to Boston, to Washington. . . . In so many cases, they did not find in the North as much as God had promised them in their dreams. But what they did find, they wanted to document since it was so often much more than what they'd had "back home" in the South. And one way of documenting it was in photos.[7]

Beginning in the 1920s, black newspapers hired photographers who could document African American life on a regional and national scale. The black community, confronting a white press that largely ignored black life and achievements, saw newspaper photography as a way to demonstrate the vitality and significance of its contributions. "No one to date has adequately explained photography's popularity in the midst of the Depression," write Pete Daniel and Sally Stein in *Official Images: New Deal Photography.* "It was an era of sacrifices, big and little, yet photographs tended to be treated as a necessity. Many felt compelled to take photographs and nearly everyone felt compelled to look at them."[8] Photography was a way for the disenfranchised to demonstrate their existence, to prove that they had a right to control their own lives. For African Americans living in a segregated Washington, photographs were indeed a "necessity."

During the 1930s and 1940s, Robert H. McNeill was a photographic chronicler of African American life in Washington, D.C. (Fig. 3.1). McNeill was truly a working photographer—constantly on the move around the capital—photographing political and social pageantry, religious and community events, and preserving a record of black neighborhoods and the world in which African Americans moved, worked, entertained, and lived (Fig. 3.2). He furnished black newspapers with a variety of images: social occasions, professional entertainers, sports figures, civil protests, political appointments. His camera enabled McNeill to get into places where a black man normally would not be allowed to enter. His attendance at the Senate hearings on the appointment of William Hastie as governor of the Virgin Islands—the first African American governor since Reconstruction—was such a significant event that McNeill himself became part of the story. The headline in the April 6, 1946, *Washington Afro-American* read: "Afro Cameraman Attends Senate Hearings on Hastie Nomination as

V.I. Governor." He also remembers taking a picture of Bill "Bojangles" Robinson from the wings of the Earle (now the Warner) Theater: "I couldn't go in the front and buy a ticket to watch the show from the audience. Yet they allowed me to take a picture from the wings" (Fig. 3.3).[9]

McNeill's photographs of Washington, D.C., in the 1930s and 1940s are successful because they portray a familiarity and comfort with their subjects. Washington was McNeill's hometown. It was where he had grown up, gone to school; he could sense the essence of people he was photographing. He shared in their successes and empathized with their despair. McNeill knew that what black Washingtonians wanted to see in the pages of their weekly newspapers was their own stories. McNeill understood this; it was his story, too.

McNeill's parents, Dr. William T. and Mary McNeill, were not native Washingtonians; both had good reasons for moving to the capital. William was born on a plantation in North Carolina but fled north to escape the racism of the South. In Washington, D.C., he enrolled at Howard Academy before attending Howard Medical School. His son remembers a dignified man, a strict but loving father. "If you'd done something that you weren't supposed to do, you knew you'd hear about it. He had a quiet way of instilling discipline."[10]

Mary McNeill went to Washington, D.C., seeking a better-paying teaching job. Her family had a more prominent position on the social register than did her husband's. "My mother was one of four children of Reverend Robert F. Wheeler of Hartford, Connecticut," the photographer recalls. "He was a friend of Mark Twain and in some way, they found that there was a society for the Worthy Coloured [that] would fund the tuition to the prestigious New England schools for these children of people who Mark Twain thought were worthy. . . . My uncle went to Harvard. My other uncle went to Springfield College, and my Aunt Laura [Wheeler Waring], the painter and portrait artist, went to the Academy of Fine Art." McNeill's mother graduated from Smith College with degrees in German and religion. In Washington, D.C., she became a teacher of German, which was taught in District public schools until the beginning of World War I.

By the second decade of the twentieth century, the promise of a life without racism that Washington, D.C., had seemed to offer the older McNeills was evaporating. But they refused to be discouraged. William McNeill became a prominent member of Washington's black leadership; his wife served on the District school board from 1926 to 1938; and they tried to shield their children from the hurt that discrimination could inflict. Robert McNeill was their third child; a brother and a sister were older. "Our parents and the society in which we lived insulated us from the realities of segregation," McNeill explains. "And because we went to segregated schools and because we went to segregated theaters and other events, we thought that was the normal thing." He remembers his mother taking him and his siblings to buy school clothes at the department stores downtown, which had segregated lunch counters. His mother would tell them:

> "Now look, we're going downtown and I want you to behave yourselves. I don't want you to touch anything. I don't want you to ask for any food. Because when we come back, I will have for you the best lunch you ever had in your life." We were anticipating this good lunch so that the hot dog counter at Woolworth's [did not tempt us at all]. We came back and sure enough, she had this salmon salad, fresh tomatoes, homemade mayonnaise and ice tea or pineapple juice. So it didn't matter. The parents took care of the situation, prepared the kids.

Although he told himself that he would follow in his father's footsteps and become a doctor, Robert McNeill's interest in photography developed early. Walking home from school, he often passed the movie theaters on U Street. "They used to put up these big displays and the glossy photographs used to be on the front of the Lincoln and Republic Theaters" (Fig. 3.4). Young Robert was, however, more interested in the photographs than the movie stars. "I used to say to myself," he remembers, "One day I want to be able to take pictures like those." He was further inspired by a photography demonstration he saw in a physics class during his sophomore or junior year in high school.

> We went into this darkroom; we were under red light. The fellow poured the chemicals into a graduate, poured them out; I could see them dissolve. He turned it over, poured the other portion to dissolve, put them in a tray, cooled it off. And then he turned the red light on and developed a roll of film in a pan. And you could see the images come out. That was fascinating; that's what probably hooked me to become a photographer. To see how that image developed on that film and how the process of development caused it to happen.

McNeill also credits a favorite aunt with encouraging him to be a photographer.

> She gave me a folding Autographic Kodak. I still have the camera. She'd taken it to Atlantic City and gotten sand in it. And she took it to one of these photo stores to see whether she could get it fixed and they said, "We can't fix it." So she gave it to me and said, "If you can fix it, you can have it." So I started banging the sand out of it, banging, and sure enough, it worked!

McNeill used the camera to take photographs for the *Dunbar Observer*, his high school paper. In fact, the 1935 Dunbar High School yearbook projects a career in photography for senior Robert McNeill. After all, he had taken pictures for the *Dunbar Observer* and published the *Officers Yearbook* with his own photographs of the cadet corps of the 1935 graduating class. Photography seemed the logical career.

But in 1935 Robert McNeill entered Howard University as a pre-med student. "In those days," he says, "you sort of figured that you'd follow in your father's footsteps, although my father and mother never insisted that we do anything of that nature. He never pushed me in that direction." McNeill's brother would become a civil engineer; his sister, a social worker. And for a while McNeill persevered with his science and Latin classes. He was on the football team and active in the drama club. He thought about becoming an actor. "They used to have these tournaments that went around the black colleges—Virginia State, Hampton, Virginia Union," he recalls. "And I was a member of the cast of a one-act play that won the tournament." But a combination of financial uncertainty and a battle with stage fright convinced him that a dramatic career was not for him.

Then, in 1936, a historic visit revived McNeill's latent passion. Jesse Owens returned to the United States in triumph after winning four gold medals at the Olympics in Berlin. Seeming to defiantly challenge Hitler's theories of a superior Aryan race, Owens was a hero to all Americans, black and white, and a symbol of inspiration to subjugated peoples all over the world. Arriving in the nation's capital, the athlete visited Howard University, and student McNeill was there to record the moment on film (Fig. 3.5). That picture, says the photographer, was "my first real success as a news photographer." It was published in the four Washington, D.C., daily papers—the *Washington Evening Star*, *Washington Daily News*, *Washington Post*, and *Washington Times-Herald*—as well as the two black papers, the *Washington Tribune* and *Washington Afro-American*. "Because of that [success]," says McNeill, "I sort of figured that [photography] was my niche in life."

In 1937 McNeill left Washington for New York to study at the New York Institute of Photography, on the way to realizing his destiny at last. "I was able to really understand that [photography] was actually what I should be doing. . . . I was on the right track," he says. During a six-month course of study at the institute, McNeill completed the commercial and the portrait courses and gained experience in photodocumentation, photographing all aspects of New York City life (Fig. 3.6). He learned about lighting and "the demeanor that's required to take portraits of people. How to handle them and how to approach them and things of that nature."

Fully confident and eagerly ready to begin a career as a photographer, McNeill returned to Washington and established a freelance photography business after spending several weeks in Virginia taking photographs for the Works Progress Administration. Initially, he worked out of his father's house on T Street; later, he founded the McNeill News Photo Service and moved to a studio on the corner of 13th and U Streets. William McNeill was fully supportive of his son's new career and even bought the young photographer a used 35 mm Contax camera for $105. He also received some "assistance" from Addison Scurlock, the famous Washington photographer who had been taking portraits of the city's black community since 1904. "Addison Scurlock gave me a break," says McNeill, laughing. "When I first went to apply for credit at Fuller and D'Albert, which was the source of photographic supplies, I gave Scurlock's name as a reference." He did that, he adds, without first obtaining the older photographer's permission. But Scurlock did not expose him to the photo supplier. "Well, he knew the family," says McNeill.

McNeill furnished pictures to several black newspapers, including the *Washington Tribune, Washington Afro-American, Philadelphia Tribune, New York Amsterdam News, Pittsburgh Courier, Norfolk Journal-Guide, Atlanta Daily World*, and *Chicago Defender*. "I was an independent freelance photographer," says Robert McNeill. "I had to buy my own film, furnish my own transportation. I did all of my darkroom work. I mailed the prints to the papers—usually by airmail. The Union Station was next to the old post office and you could run down there any time, day or night, and get the pictures off." For the most part, editors did not formally assign a photographer to a particular event; they depended on their freelancers to know what was happening around the city, to be on the scene, and to provide a shot that would be of interest to their readers. "It was a natural, human-interest thing," says McNeill. "They were looking for pictures of people and they were trying to increase circulation." Whether or not the newspapers bought prints depended on the significance of the event to the African American community. "If it was something very [important], like the integration of the golf course, they were interested. I wouldn't just limit [myself] to one paper; I'd service the *Washington Tribune* and if it had some national significance, I'd send it out to six or seven black newspapers on the east coast."

McNeill often served as reporter as well as photographer, providing extensive captions for the editors' benefit. A lyrical image of a multiple baptism by Pentecostal minister Daddy Grace, for instance, bears the following legend: "Immersed in the water up to his arm-pits for two hours and a half, 'Daddy' Grace baptized more than two hundred converts as his assistants led them to him and helped them to the dressing rooms, carried away by religious ecstacy [sic]. The small band at the right played rhythmic spirituals and blues continuously, adding to the emotional fervor" (Fig. 3.7). McNeill's captions often provided out-of-town editors with the complete story. For example, for a photograph of the opening of the Washington bureau of the National Association for the Advancement of Colored People he wrote this caption: "Showing that the Capitol Building is only a stone's throw from the Bureau's offices at 100 Massachusetts Avenue [are] Frank Reeves, bureau chief, and Walter White, secretary of the National Association." The Capitol building to which Reeves is pointing cannot be seen in the photograph (Fig. 3.8).

The late 1930s was a dynamic time for a young photographer working on his own. "I was busy all the time," McNeill recalls. "I scratched out a living. During that time, I probably reported an income of about $1,900 [a year]." Although Franklin Delano Roosevelt had been sworn into presidential office in 1933 promising a New Deal, African Americans had seen few benefits. While New Deal programs revitalized Washington's white commercial entities, the resulting prosperity did not trickle down to black businesses; problems with housing and the public school system remained much the same. It was a time of turmoil, nationally and internationally. News of the Nazi Party's racially based policies in Germany were causing Americans to take a second look at discrimination in the United States. African Americans were publicly and vocally asserting their civil rights as they had not done since Reconstruction.

Then, early in 1939, as Constance McLaughlin Green writes in *The Secret City*, the

national limelight suddenly focused on racial discrimination in the capital when the D.A.R. [Daughters of the American Revolution] refused to allow the famous contralto Marian Anderson to sing in the D.A.R.-owned Constitution Hall. . . . The furor aroused in the city and throughout the country exceeded any outburst of indignation within the memory of Washington's oldest inhabitants. White people were jolted out of their assumption that Negroes with ambition and talent could make their way anywhere, for here was a woman of utmost distinction being treated as an obnoxious nonentity. Marian Anderson revealed to the nation the depths into which white ignorance and prejudice had forced all Negroes.[11]

Eleanor Roosevelt resigned from the DAR, and the situation was volatile until Harold Ickes, the secretary of the interior, invited Anderson to sing at the Lincoln Memorial.

Seventy-five thousand people gathered around the memorial to hear Marian Anderson sing on that Easter Sunday in 1939. The incident became a symbol for black Washingtonians and African Americans all over the United States, McNeill believes, because Marian Anderson

was considered to be one of the top contraltos. She'd been exalted, hailed, and honored by the Europeans. She could sing in Europe without any question whatsoever. She sang at Carnegie Hall; she sang at all the other places and for them to say [it was] because she was black was the highest insult of all. It wasn't because she wasn't a good singer; it was because she was black. And of course, those were fighting words.

Washington's seventy-year-old fight against discrimination "was no longer a local affair only. Race relations in the capital were thenceforward a matter of interest to Americans everywhere."[12]

The event, which attracted the attention of men, women, and children nationwide, must have been covered by every reporter and photographer in the city. As always, McNeill rushed from the memorial to his darkroom to the post office to airmail his photographs of the concert to black newspapers around the country. "There was a difference between taking pictures today and then," he explains.

We had to remember to open the camera; had to pull the lens out on a track until it was in proper position. [Then we would] open the back to look at the ground glass, and focus and set the diaphragm, cock the shutter, insert the film holder, pull the slide and compose the picture in the view finder. And then take the picture. I counted once; I think it was an 11-step process. I used to put a checklist on my camera [so that I would remember everything].

It was a mad rush to get everything finished. But McNeill then fell victim to the perils that came with being an independent photographer with limited access to new technologies. "I covered [Marian Anderson's performance] for several of the newspapers," he says, "including my cousin's paper in Wilmington, North Carolina. [But] some of the papers had received the pictures from the wire services so they returned my picture [saying] thanks, but they hadn't gotten mine in time." Readers in North Carolina, however, did see McNeill's photograph of Marian Anderson and Harold Ickes; it was published in his cousin's paper (Fig. 3.9).

A democracy cannot survive unless it produces a citizenry properly developed so that it can and will take an intelligent, active part in important issues in the state, nation and world. Our education must, therefore, produce an intelligent, responsible, and participating citizenry. A citizen cannot function intelligently in a democratic society unless he is accurately informed concerning the problems and contributions of all members of that society. This correct information will make for tolerance and sympathetic understanding among the members.

—John C. Bruce
Journal of Negro History 22 (1937)

Since black contributions were not taught in the public school system in the 1930s and 1940s, "Negro history" continued to come under the purview of the media. McNeill's images helped Washington's black newspapers encourage and inspire their readers to action and reaction. Pictures of entertainers and political activists helped to reassure African Americans that a successful future was more than probable, it was a certainty. Some of the events and figures McNeill photographed are household names to us today: Joe Louis, the heavyweight champion from 1937 to 1949, out of character in a baseball uniform (Fig. 3.10); Duke Ellington on a national tour; Ralph Bunche; Hattie McDaniel; Ella Fitzgerald (Fig. 3.11); Jackie Robinson in town for the all-star game at Griffiths Stadium; Lionel Hampton; Eleanor and Franklin Roosevelt.

In McNeill's photographs, however, it is the black community of Washington, D.C., that plays a central role. In one image, of a 1941 Joe Louis fight, his focus is not on the two boxers, but on Louis being examined by Dr. Herbert Marshall, a prominent District physician and the son of an equally well known doctor (Fig. 3.12). In the newspaper pages, Duke Ellington is portrayed as a local boy on a hometown visit. Such photographs of the famous are the ones McNeill knew would be bought by the editors. He meets his subjects head-on; they take up the entire frame of the picture. Nothing distracts from the main event.

McNeill's images establish that, as the years went by, the African American community was beginning to attract the attention of white Washington society. They depict Franklin Roosevelt speaking at a Howard University commencement, Eleanor Roosevelt dedicating a Police Boys Club (Fig. 3.13), the federal judge William Hastie being confirmed as governor of the Virgin Islands. In a 1946 photograph of Mary Church Terrell addressing the National Association of Colored Women, McNeill also captures a white photographer adjusting his camera, preparing to take his own picture of the occasion (Fig. 3.14). The white media had begun to realize that there was another world out there to cover as African Americans began to make their presence known (Fig. 3.15).

African American editors and publishers realized that no accomplishment was achieved easily; therefore, every success, every struggle, was considered big news. McNeill's photographs usually adhered to the newspapers' policies of exposing discrimination and Jim Crowism and fighting for equality at all levels. They include the 1940 opening of the T Street post office, the first in the city with an all-black staff (Fig. 3.16); picketers marching in front of Safeway supermarkets and People's drugstores because management refused to hire black clerks in stores in black neighborhoods;[13] African American men and women demonstrating their ability and desire to join the war effort; Chicago taxi drivers gathering in the capital city to expose discriminatory hiring practices; members of the National Association of Colored Women outside the White House, protesting a lynching in Georgia (Fig. 3.17). McNeill's images of a Washington, D.C., at the forefront of the civil rights movement appeared in newspapers around the country.

One of McNeill's photographs for a local newspaper was of a woman nearly blinded by a nurse who accidentally put alcohol into her eye. The woman, Anesta Foster, sits on a park bench, wearing a pair of sunglasses. A second photograph, a close-up of her face without the sunglasses, reveals a young woman, probably in her early twenties, shyly smiling. Looking at her demure, unthreatening expression, the reader cannot help but feel relief at her near escape. But read on; Miss Foster's situation is only part of the story. "We suggest," writes the reporter, "that the Government might do well to change its policy of selection, and employ people in responsible categories on the basis of merit and efficiency, and not exclude others on the basis of color who are capable and careful."[14]

Now as everyone knows, Howard University is the capstone of Negro education in the world. There gather Negro money, beauty, and prestige. It is to the Negro what Harvard is to the whites. They say the same thing about a Howard man that they do about Harvard—you can tell a Harvard man as far as you can see him, but you can't tell him much. He listens to the doings of other Negro schools and their graduates with bored tolerance. Not only is the scholastic rating at Howard high, but tea is poured in the manner!

—Zora Neale Hurston
Dust Tracks on a Road: An Autobiography (1942)

McNeill's photographs of Washington life tell a story of a strong and determined African American community. Segregation was an evil to be fought and conquered, but in the meantime, black people formed their own organizations: black YWCAs and YMCAs, black Boy Scout and Girl Scout troupes (Fig. 3.18), even an African American Junior League. McNeill was there to record each special occasion. "People would give me tips and leads; knowing that I was a photographer, they'd call me up," he says. His images portray an African American community that always worked together, united in the struggle for civil rights and unaware of class differences. But this was not the reality. In Washington, D.C., "rigid class distinctions still prevailed within the [black] community. At Howard University, the scions of the cave dwellers looked down their patrician noses at black classmates from other parts of the country or from the lower ranks of local society."[15] As McNeill remembers today, Rayford Logan, Alain Locke, Sterling Brown, and the other distinguished faculty at Howard University "lived in a sort of preserved, protected enclave. They came and went in the Howard University atmosphere; the people that they saw were people that were brought in from the outside." This is the world that was published in the pages of the *Washington Tribune*, the *Washington Afro-American*, and other black newspapers. Weddings and cotillions, award ceremonies and graduations, meetings and conferences, protests and political activities—these were the subjects in which the newspapers were interested. And these were images that Robert McNeill provided.

But McNeill was also curious about his own world, about the iceman who came to the house and the laborers who worked for the moving companies. They—as well as boys reading comic books in the street (Fig. 3.19), workers at the corner market (Fig. 3.20), hairdressers at the local beauty shop (Fig. 3.21)—all became subjects for McNeill's camera. In 1942 he was drafted into the army and stationed in Alabama and on Guadalcanal, but he kept right on taking pictures. As a result, McNeill created a rich and personal photographic record of army life during World War II. His images of army dances seem almost multidimensional, full of excitement, sound, and movement. A few years later, he traveled for the United Negro College Fund (UNCF), taking photographs at the eleven member colleges that had established programs for World War II veterans. "The contract," McNeill remembers, "called for 1,100 negatives so they could use them in their permanent file for publicity purposes." But McNeill worked beyond the scope of the contract, providing detailed captions and notes that chronicle educational, cultural, and sports activities at UNCF colleges during the 1940s.

Robert H. McNeill was not just a newspaper photographer; he was a recorder of history at a time when black newspapers were making a concerted effort to document the accomplishments and contributions of their community. His images of Washington, D.C., during the 1930s and 1940s will forever transport us back to a complex world where African Americans struggling for civil rights used

every resource available. Some were peaceful and passive, like the continuing desire for education and the calculated use of votes. Some were peaceful and active, like the push to break down labor union and employment barriers and the play to get more national publicity. . . . American society could no longer sit back, consoled by the thought that the Negro was not yet prepared. [H]e was ready, and in the decade to come, the young men and women of his race would make this clear.[16]

Notes

1. Michael Andrew Fitzpatrick, "A Great Agitation for Business: Black Economic Development in Shaw," *Washington History* 1, no. 2 (fall/winter 1990–91): p. 55.
2. Willard B. Gatewood, *Aristocrats of Color: The Black Elite, 1880–1920* (Bloomington: Indiana University Press, 1990), p. 334.
3. David L. Lewis, *District of Columbia: A Bicentennial History* (New York: W. W. Norton & Company and the American Association for State and Local History, 1976), p. 72.
4. Nancy J. Weiss, "The Negro and the New Freedom," in *The Segregation Era, 1863–1954*, ed. Allen Weinstein and Frank Otto Gatell (New York: Oxford University Press, 1970), p. 131.
5. Fitzpatrick, "A Great Agitation for Business," p. 73.
6. Marcia M. Greenlee, "Shaw," in *Washington at Home: An Illustrated History of Neighborhoods in the Nation's Capital*, ed. Kathryn Schneider Smith (Washington, D.C.: Windsor Publications, 1988), p. 124.
7. Edward P. Jones, "A Sunday Portrait," in *Picturing Us: African American Identity in Photography*, ed. Deborah Willis (New York: New Press, 1994), p. 36.
8. Pete Daniel and Sally Stein, introduction to *Official Images: New Deal Photography*, ed. Daniel and Stein (Washington, D.C.: Smithsonian Institution Press, 1987), p. viii.
9. This and all subsequent quotes from Robert H. McNeill are from interviews conducted by the author on April 26, 1993, and March 14, 1995, except where noted.
10. Robert H. McNeill, interview by Ed Smith, Anacostia Museum, Washington, D.C., 1990, videocassette.
11. Constance McLaughlin Green, *The Secret City: A History of Race Relations in the Nation's Capital* (Princeton, N.J.: Princeton University Press, 1967), pp. 248–49.
12. Ibid., p. 249.
13. For many years Safeway refused to hire black clerks, even in black neighborhoods. Beginning in the 1930s and into the 1940s, the New Negro Alliance and the NAACP organized boycotts of Safeway, People's, and other shops with discriminatory practices. Many stores eventually chose to integrate rather than incur economic losses.
14. "Careless Nurse Nearly Blinds Clerk," *Sentry*, August 1, 1942, p. 3.

15. Green, *The Secret City*, p. 250.

16. Leslie H. Fishel Jr. and Benjamin Quarles, "In the New Deal's Wake," in *The Segregation Era, 1863–1954*, ed. Weinstein and Gatell, p. 232.

3.1 Robert H. McNeill, *Camera for Sale: Self-Portrait*, 1940. This photograph won a prize in *Popular Photography*'s picture contest, September 1940. Courtesy of Robert H. McNeill, Washington, D.C.

3.2 Robert H. McNeill, *The Capitol Press Club*. The Capitol Press Club was an all-black organization of men and women who worked in the news. Robert McNeill is in the top left corner. Courtesy of Robert H. McNeill, Washington, D.C.

3.3 Robert H. McNeill, *Bill "Bojangles" Robinson at the Earle Theater,* late 1930s. Courtesy of Robert H. McNeill, Washington, D.C.

3.4 Robert H. McNeill, *The Republic Theater at Night,* 1940s, Washington, D.C. Prior to the 1950s, Washington's movie theaters were segregated. Several that served the African American community were black–owned, but the Republic, which catered to a black clientele and had a black staff, was operated by the District Theater chain, headed by white businessman Abraham E. Lichtman. Courtesy of Robert H. McNeill, Washington, D.C.

3.5 Robert H. McNeill, *Jesse Owens and Mordecai Johnson*, Howard University's President, at Howard University, 1937. This photograph of Jesse Owens, center, visiting Howard University after his triumph at the 1936 Olympics was bought by all the Washington newspapers, black and white. Johnson is pictured at his right. The success encouraged McNeill to become a photographer. Courtesy of Robert H. McNeill, Washington, D.C.

3.6 Robert H. McNeill, *Jitterbug, Savoy Ballroom*, ca. 1937. Courtesy of Robert H. McNeill, Washington, D.C.

3.7 Robert H. McNeill, *Daddy Grace Baptism: In the Water*, 1949. Bishop Marcelino Manoel de Graca, "Daddy Grace," was a charismatic leader who attracted thousands of followers to his Pentecostal church during the 1930s and 1940s, promising salvation and providing jobs and economic empowerment. Courtesy of Robert H. McNeill, Washington, D.C.

3.8 Robert H. McNeill, *Frank Reeves, Bureau Chief, and Walter White, National Secretary, outside the National Association for the Advancement of Colored People's New Washington Offices,* 1940s. Courtesy of Robert H. McNeill, Washington, D.C.

3.9 Robert H. McNeill, *Harold L. Ickes and Marian Anderson*, 1939. Schomburg Center for Research in Black Culture, New York Public Library.

Art Center College

3.10 Robert H. McNeill, *Joe Louis in Softball Uniform*, 1930s, New York. Jesse Owens, Jackie Robinson, and Joe Louis were all considered heroes by the African American community because of their achievements in the sports world and the symbols they became in the civil rights movement. Yet, when he was not boxing, Louis toured the country with a softball team, a publicity stunt organized by his managers. "They exploited these guys," says Robert McNeill. Courtesy of Robert H. McNeill, Washington, D.C.

3.11 Robert H. McNeill, *Ella Fitzgerald and the Philip Morris Man*, 1930s. Courtesy of Robert H. McNeill, Washington, D.C.

3.12 Robert H. McNeill, *Dr. Herbert Marshall Examining Joe Louis before the Boxer's Fight with Billy Conn*, 1941. Courtesy of Robert H. McNeill, Washington, D.C.

3.13 Robert H. McNeill, *Eleanor Roosevelt Dedicating the Police Boys Club in Washington's Number Two Precinct,* ca. 1936. Two boys' clubs were established in 1934 by the chief of police, who thought they would combat juvenile delinquency; but they were for white boys only. A separate club for black boys was opened in 1936. Courtesy of Robert H. McNeill, Washington, D.C.

3.14 Robert H. McNeill, *Mary Church Terrell Addressing Members of the National Association of Colored Women at Their Golden Jubilee,* 1946. Courtesy of Robert H. McNeill, Washington, D.C.

3.15 Robert H. McNeill, *Outside the Capitol,* n.d. Courtesy of Robert H. McNeill, Washington, D.C.

3.16 Robert H. McNeill, *Opening of the T Street Post Office*, 1940. This was the first post office with an all-black staff in Washington, D.C. The opening was an important story in the city's black newspapers. Courtesy of Robert H. McNeill, Washington, D.C.

3.17 Robert H. McNeill, *National Association of Colored Women Members March outside the White House to Protest a Lynching in Georgia*, 1946. Five hundred NACW delegates, from every state, participated in the march. Courtesy of Robert H. McNeill, Washington, D.C.

3.18 Robert H. McNeill, *Girl Scout Cookout.* Courtesy of Robert H. McNeill, Washington, D.C.

3.19 Robert H. McNeill, *Boys Reading Comic Books*. Courtesy of Robert H. McNeill, Washington, D.C.

3.20 Robert H. McNeill, *We Sell the Best*, 1940. The caption that accompanied this photograph in the November 16, 1940, edition of the *Washington Tribune* read: "This quintet mans the modern branch of the Table Supply Stores, located at 2007 Fourteenth Street, Northwest. Pictured left to right are: Lawrence Jones, Henry Hiel, Charles Boyd, Harry Green, and Douglas Williams, manager." Courtesy of Robert H. McNeill, Washington, D.C.

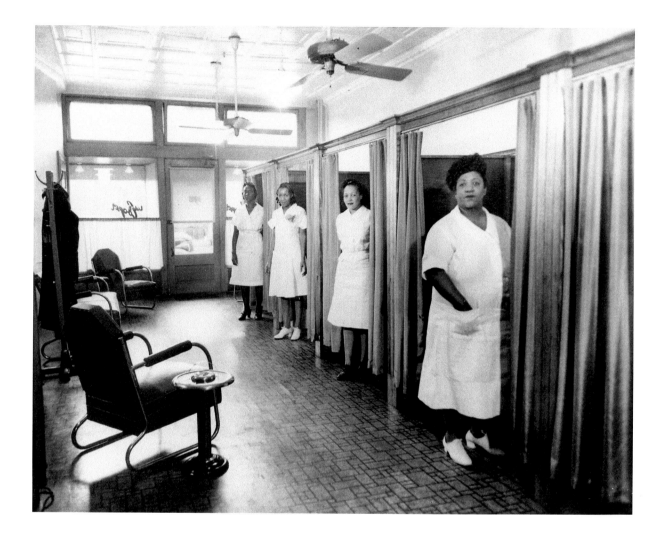

3.21 Robert H. McNeill, *Lula B. Cooper French Beauty Salon*, ca. 1939, Washington, D.C. Courtesy of Robert H. McNeill, Washington, D.C.

4. ROBERT H. MCNEILL AND THE PROFUSION OF VIRGINIA EXPERIENCE

Nicholas Natanson

Following are the memories of a New Deal era black government photographer at work, first, in his office and, next, on the road and, finally, serving in the military during wartime:

As I sat down to talk to the [editors] about the assignment, I had the impression they wanted noncontroversial photos. You know, "don't rock the boat." Nobody ever told me not to rock the boat, but that was what I sensed. They wanted fairly positive pictures. . . . If I had focused on the more political [topics], the photos would have been filtered out by the editors; they didn't want to seem too partisan.

I was driving this Ford black coupe, with "USA" on the license plate. As I pulled into the coal town, this sheriff with a long gun going practically to his knee, stopped me and started in with, "Boy, what are you doing with this USA car?" He emphasized the "boy" and the "USA." I gave him the logical explanation, and he was still suspicious. "Well, I got to check into that!" So I was taken to the sheriff's office, and they telegraphed the [headquarters] office to investigate. Found out I was telling the truth . . . but they never did let me photograph in the mines. Only the show mine.

Out on my first leave, as a first sergeant in the army, I took a train to Birmingham, and when we arrived, there were these MPs with billy clubs, shunting us off to the black waiting room. Guys had to restrain me as I was voicing my outrage. "Here we are, fighting for democracy, fighting against Hitler, and look what we're getting here in Birmingham!" I didn't have my camera. I wish I had![1]

It would be easy to assume that these memories belong to Gordon Parks, the adventurous photographer often celebrated as the lone pioneer, the only African American cameraman in the civilian sector of the federal government during the depression and World War II. Parks, after all, had his start in Roy Stryker's Farm Security Administration (FSA) Historical Section, the documentary photography unit that has drawn the lion's share of scholarly and popular attention over the years. And, after all, most current photo-historians, critical of what is often considered the "middle-class" direction of FSA leadership, are fond of imagining Parks, along with pioneering FSA women photographers, contending not only with the forces of reaction in the countryside but with an allegedly restrictive, bureaucratic Stryker.[2]

So much for easy assumptions. The memories are those of Robert H. McNeill, who spent the better part of September 1938 traveling the length and breadth of Virginia, documenting black life for the Works Progress Administration Federal Writers' Project publication *The Negro in Virginia*.[3] Four years before Parks's oft-chronicled arrival at the FSA, McNeill was very much the trailblazer, confronting myriad political, administrative, aesthetic, and practical challenges as a twenty-year-old black man journeying, essentially on his own, through a state that he had never visited before. Too often forgotten in later years, the McNeill investigation produced a photographic record that adds new dimensions to our understanding of the photographic implications of the outsider as insider, the black documentarian as government-sponsored documentarian.

To be sure, there are *other* too-often-forgotten African American photographic connections to the government in this era. James Stephen Wright, who could only be hired as a "photographer assistant" when he joined the Public Works Administration in 1935, quietly managed to have the job title reversed, and by the turn of the 1940s, he was heading the entire Federal Works Agency (FWA) Photo Section. Randolph MacDougall joined Wright and five white photographers on a racially integrated FWA staff. Roger Smith, brought into the Office of War Information (OWI) in late 1942 to photograph for the Negro Press Section, was frequently credited as the "Official OWI Negro Photographer" in black newspapers. Emmanuel F. Joseph performed defense-related contract assignments for the OWI on the West Coast. Aubrey Pollard, who would later work for McNeill in the private sector, contributed to Federal Arts Project documentary photography undertakings in New York City in the late 1930s.[4] In short, neither Gordon Parks nor Robert McNeill was alone.

But McNeill's Virginia experience is especially significant, not only because of the richness both of the images and of his testimony about the images in recent years. The nature of his mission moved beyond the predictable recording of New Deal and defense program achievements that tended to characterize the work of Wright, MacDougall, Smith, and Joseph, and bore intriguing parallels with better-known FSA ventures. As well, McNeill's own nongovernment and, later, government pursuits (with Wright at the State Department, from 1956 to 1976) help to place the Virginia production in further perspective.

As we will see, the story of McNeill's work for *The Negro in Virginia* involved not simply a collision of black interests with white middle-class conventions—the sort of 1930s cultural scenario favored by photo-historians of late—but a more complex interplay of a young photographer's curiosities, black educational establishment agendas, the needs of government officials white and black, and the varied choices of photographic subjects. It is a story of McNeill's quiet resistance to many of what historian Edward Ayers would call the "totalizing metaphors" of an era.[5] And it is a story of McNeill's partial innovations: creativity not without elements of accommodation, and creative possibilities not always fully realized.

In approaching the work of McNeill, it is important to avoid the mistake made by recent critics of FSA photography, namely, disregarding the larger world of visual choices made by other photographers, government and nongovernment, in the thirties and forties. Photographic depictions of African Americans during this period tended to fall into distinct genres.

Prominent was the Colorful Black, seen frequently in the white-edited mass media, in forms varying from watermelon-eaters and cotton-patch snoozers to high-spirited military enlistees. There was the Noble Primitive, central to Doris Ulmann's precapitalist visions, some of Aaron Siskind's poetic Harlem visions, and Works Progress Administration staff photographer Oscar Jordan's New Deal diversions (for example, his 1938 view of black WPA laborers in Georgia singing spirituals while they work [Fig. 4.1]). On the other extreme lay the Black Victim, sufficiently pathetic, in the Margaret Bourke-White renderings, to invite associations with the old colorful stereotypes. There was the Transformed Black, with a dehumanized "before" giving way to an artificial "after," as in the standard U.S. Housing Authority (USHA) photographic juxtapositions.[6]

And, especially in the black press, there appeared the glittering Role Model, the polished professional whose visual authority was designed to counter the effect of many of the aforementioned representational modes. While black journalistic text often exposed injustice, visuals tended overwhelmingly to be upbeat. Thus, in a 1938 issue of the *Norfolk Journal-Guide*, a hard-hitting textual investigation of conditions for black domestics ran alongside a prominent photo-feature on the well-appointed home of a Virginia black landowner.[7] Consistent in many respects with this black newspaper pictorial tradition were the earnest "national contributor" visions in government war information photography of the 1940s. "Of course these pictures weren't telling the full story," remembered Jewell Mazique, a Washington, D.C., government worker who was the subject of a cheery government photo-story in 1942. "But if a photographer was trying to break down the stereotypes of us as crude and ignorant and lazy, if he was trying to show us closing the gap between former slaves and former masters, I was going to cooperate."[8]

It was within the subculture of successful black professionals, the very sort so frequently pictured in black newspapers, that McNeill grew up, son of a physician and a school administrator in Washington, D.C. In the world of McNeill's youth, the very notion of making a career of photography, as opposed to medicine or education or the ministry, represented a mild rebellion. McNeill's movement outward proceeded gradually, but by the late 1930s the one-time camera tinkerer had become an aspiring camera professional at Howard University, thinking critically about photographic convention.

> The Scurlock Studio had this big display case that was like a feature page of a newspaper, with all kinds of significant events and people [depicted]—weddings, graduations, first black at the Naval Academy, and so forth. What characterized that stuff was that everything look so posed, so unreal. The photographer was so busy making sure that the pictures were flattering, that everything looked like everything else. At that point, I was devouring every photography magazine I could get my hands on, and I was seeing other possibilities . . . Cartier-Bresson, Capa, *Life* stories, the FSA group. I was struck by the contrasts in those FSA photos—the [John Vachon] picture with the Capitol dome overlooking the littered slum streets. I made up my mind that I was going to be a documentarian.[9]

Flash!, a black-published, Washington, D.C.–based picture magazine that combined elements of traditional black photojournalism with more inventive documentary forays, provided an initial venue for McNeill's experimentation, including work done outside the nation's capital.[10] While a student at the New York Institute of Photography in November 1937, McNeill received a tip that the New York–based *Fortune* needed photos of the domestic workers, mostly black, who assembled on designated street corners each day to sell their labor to the highest bidder (Figs. 4.2–4.4). McNeill acted quickly. Five years before Gordon Parks produced his now famous photo-story on the government charwoman Ella Watson, McNeill was following Bessie Windstown from the long wait on the corner of 170th Street and Walton Avenue in the Bronx to an employer's kitchen.

The *Bronx Slave Market* photo-story employed ironic placements that recalled the FSA's Arthur Rothstein and anticipated Parks: one group of job seekers stands near an advertisement for the movie *Make a Wish*. It also employed tense juxtapositions and elliptical touches that recalled Ben Shahn's FSA picture-story on Arkansas cotton pickers reproduced in *Flash!*. A white housewife and black domestic negotiate the day's wage, with a literal and figurative space between them; and a job seeker's scrawled note on a wall offers a tenuous affirmation of selfhood amid an environment overwhelmingly hostile to selfhood. *Bronx Slave Market* also utilized unsettling spatial effects that paralleled those used in the roughly contemporaneous Photo League project, *Harlem Document*. Windstown, on hands and knees scrubbing the floor, is photographed from a low angle that seems to propel her work into the viewer's space.[11] As McNeill recalled:

> It was the small things that struck me. . . . How cold it was on that particular morning on that particular corner in the Bronx. The idea that this woman had come up from the South, maybe was staying with relatives in New York and needed to help pay the rent, and ended up doing what she had known in the South. Or the expression on the white woman's face, after she offers to pay 15 cents [an hour] and [Windstown] says, "Uh-uh, 20 cents is my price." I guess the pictures were too strong for *Fortune*, though, because they were never used.[12]

As its title, "The Servant Problem," would suggest, the article that *Fortune* ultimately published in early 1938 was composed entirely from the employer's vantage point and had little room for Bessie Windstown.[13] *Fortune's* rejection became a major, thirteen-photo *Flash!* feature. *Flash!* publisher Dutton Ferguson's accompanying narrative had its occasional sensationalistic excesses, but the spread nevertheless did qualitative and quantitative justice to McNeill's original series.[14]

The exposure in *Flash!* helped remind one of McNeill's Howard University contacts, writer and literary critic Sterling Brown, of the photographer's talents. It was Brown who opened the door to McNeill's Virginia venture. As editor in Negro Affairs at the headquarters office of the Federal Writers' Project (FWP), Brown helped launch in 1937 what was to become *The Negro in Virginia*, one of more than a dozen such black-oriented state and local history undertakings by assorted Writers' Project units in the late 1930s.[15] These black studies resulted in part from the ethnic and racial interests of FWP national director Henry Alsberg, in part from the forceful lobbying of Brown and such state WPA black advisors as Virginia's Thomas H. Walker, and in part from the predictable resistance of most southern state guide editors to the employment of black field-workers for—and to any significant inclusion of black material within—the general state publications. With the notable exception of the Washington, D.C., guide, which included Brown's lengthy and probing chapter on black life, southern state guides tended to devote only a few pages to sections with titles such as "Negroes," with pictorial black representation sparse at best.[16]

The special Virginia project afforded rare opportunities for an all-black staff to work under the day-to-day direction of a black writer-editor, Hampton Institute science professor Roscoe Lewis. Although by no means an established writer, Lewis, an old friend of Brown's, had the planning, coordinating, and synthesizing skills necessary for a publication project with such a varied agenda. The book aimed to reach back to the very beginnings of Virginia history, correcting myths about the meaning and impact of slavery; it also aimed to reach forward to the New Deal era, exploring the political, social, and cultural status of present-day black Virginians. Making use of oral testimony (the Virginia portion of the now famous former-slave narratives), the project also cast its research net more widely than such works as the Georgia Federal Writers' Project's *Drums and Shadows*, based exclusively on interviews.[17] At the same time, *The Negro in Virginia* was not created in a political or administrative void, and Lewis found his considerable diplomatic skills tested.

Lewis's drafts were reviewed carefully by, among others, Virginia Writers' Project director Eudora Ramsay Richardson, a self-styled white progressive who worried about white reaction to the eventual publication. Objecting to some of Lewis's grim characterizations of slave life, Richardson complained to Alsberg: "After all, the book will have the stamp of the Federal Writers' Project and will come out of Virginia. So we must proceed cautiously and with fairness to both Negroes and whites. The Negroes would defeat their own purpose should the book appear in print as it is now written."[18]

Lewis, desperately needing Richardson's and Alsberg's support to gain the full staffing that the black project was originally promised, could not afford to ignore such pressures.[19] Nor could state and national Writers' Project administrators afford to ignore the rumblings from Congress.

At the time of textual editing and visual planning for *The Negro in Virginia*, in late summer of 1938, the Dies Committee opened its highly publicized investigations into radical influence in the Writers' Project and the Theater Project. With the Dies hearings giving way the following year to the equally hostile inquiries of the Woodrum Committee, headed by Virginia's own powerful Clifton Woodrum, the attacks continued through much of the period of final manuscript preparation.[20] While race did not figure as the central focus of the Dies or Woodrum hearings, it often lurked behind the Communist subversion issue. One Dies witness, quoted in the press, charged that Writers' Project headquarters personnel had reinserted into the Tennessee guide copy that, rejected by state authorities, included "10 or 15 pages of instructions as to the Negro's rights and their [sic] labor troubles." Another witness averred that the same national officials "often build up a case for the Negro where none is necessary. There has always been an effort to build up subtly the oppression of the Negro everywhere, in every copy."[21]

Like other Writers' Project productions, *The Negro in Virginia* needed official institutional sponsorship, with its assurance of future book sales, to attract a commercial publisher; and Lewis, under considerable pressure from Richardson, spent much time in 1937 and 1938 trying to arrange sponsorship with one or more of Virginia's black colleges. Sponsorship had very definite manuscript content implications, as Richardson assured Hampton Institute's white president, Arthur Howe, in May 1938. "The directors of the Federal Writers' Project agreed to furnish the sponsors with a full copy of the manuscript and to make such changes, deletions, or additions as the sponsors may deem necessary."[22]

Howe, who made Hampton library facilities available to the Writers' Project from the very beginning and who later agreed to make Hampton the sole sponsor of *The Negro in Virginia*, had his own narrative agenda that centered on affirmation, inspiration, and racial cooperation. As he wrote Alsberg:

> Most of the history textbooks used in our [nation's] schools and even in our colleges make some brief reference to a certain number of slaves, but say very little about the skills and the improvement, and the outstanding records this minority group has made in the comparatively short period since Emancipation. If American democracy is going to prove to the world that a minority group can live happily and become part of a great people, it is only going to be accomplished by very much greater efforts in educating members of the white majority group.[23]

Amid these pressures, subtle and not so subtle, Lewis fashioned a text that offered a basic narrative of hope—the tribulations of slavery, the struggles and the progress of the decades since, the promise of the future—with a more meditative undercurrent suggesting the continuing burden of inequality, poverty, and ignorance, and the persistence of racial misperceptions. As Lewis cautioned potential white readers in a passage that made it into print, "No matter how carefree the outward appearance of Negroes may be, behind their outward masks are poverty, disease, and suffering, inherent in the existence of a people relegated to a neglected, segregated, and economically precarious way of life."[24]

The various editorial reworkings by Alsberg and Brown in Washington, D.C., and by Richardson, Howe, and white historian John Russell in Virginia, did not eliminate this undercurrent, but they did serve to bolster the more sanguine dimensions of the text. It was no coincidence that passages were added emphasizing black home- and land-ownership gains in the twentieth century.[25] Nor was it coincidental, in light of the administrative pressures, that some of the more detailed and arresting examples of discrimination explored in Lewis's research notes never reached the final publication. They included the banning of a prominent black player from Virginia collegiate baseball; the erection of a "county" training school for blacks, with the county contributing but one hundred dollars to a total cost of ten thousand dollars; and low black-voting percentages for specific Virginia cities.[26]

National and state administrators had always tacitly assumed that the black Virginia publication would incorporate an important visual component. Still, most of the Virginia photographic planning was devoted to the general state guide, under preparation at roughly the same time as *The Negro in Virginia* and also published in 1940.[27] Alsberg and Richardson arranged for W. Lincoln Highton, a WPA staff cameraman specializing in guide work, to photograph in Virginia in the summer of 1938. Highton, the assumption went, would concentrate mainly on his customary scenic landscapes, architectural studies, and local-color views for the state guide, and would also provide, along the way, some black-related material to illustrate the contemporary life chapters of *The Negro in Virginia*. Highton's eventual output did include some scattered black subjects, typified by views of a church exterior, an old porch sitter taking in the late afternoon sun, and a daffodil seller whose countenance seems to absorb the warm glow of the flowers.[28]

Richardson found Highton's placid pictures "just what we need for the Negro book."[29] But Brown, Alsberg, and Lewis wanted something more. Content considerations, as well as Lewis's continuing emphasis on black contributions to the publication, prompted alternative thinking. "Undoubtedly," an Alsberg assistant noted on August 11, "it will be necessary to send a Negro photographer through Virginia to get . . . the human interest pictures that are wanted."[30] That opened the door for McNeill, whose appointment in late August was publicized in Virginia's leading black newspaper, the *Norfolk Journal-Guide*.[31] Recalled McNeill:

The feeling was that the Highton stuff was too stilted, too commercial. So Brown contacted me and suggested I go see Alsberg, and I took along some of my work to show what I could do. From then on, things started rolling. I was brought on as a [per diem] photographic consultant, and by the end of August I was sitting down with Lewis talking about the job. There were no written guidelines or scripts, but I understood what they wanted were pictures of people at work, pictures that would show the soul of people in their jobs . . . and the dignity, even for people in menial occupations. The idea was to show that people hadn't given up. I was given a deadline; I was given some supplies and some contacts in Virginia; and I was given a car. And I was elated.[32]

The Virginia to which the twenty-year-old was introduced—beginning in Richmond, then traveling south to Norfolk and Portsmouth, west toward Roanoke, and on to the West Virginia border—posed many of the sights that his mother had tried to shield from him in earlier years. Segregation, inscribed in state and local law, held sway as firmly in most areas of depression-era Virginia as it did in the Deep South. "Not that I was necessarily looking for it, but it was part of a place like Richmond, part of a lot of places in Virginia," McNeill remembered. "I was aware of it again in the war years, after I finished officer training and was sent to Camp Lee, Virginia. They had this sham of a welcoming booth set up for the new arrivals, one side marked 'white,' the other side 'colored.' The people serving in the booth would just go back and forth from one side to the other—a complete farce!"[33] For all the black success stories carefully chronicled by Lewis in *The Negro in Virginia* text, poverty remained the common condition for Virginia blacks. Rooted in processes and structures that pre-dated the depression, problems of low wages, agricultural tenancy, unemployment and underemployment, and inadequate housing were only exacerbated by the general economic downturns of the 1930s, including the 1937–1938 recession out of which Virginia was struggling at the time of McNeill's visit.

This was a state where two-thirds of rural black households had annual incomes of less than six hundred dollars, where upwards of 80 percent of urban black households had annual incomes of less than one thousand dollars, and where in most cities more than half the black-occupied dwellings were classified by the federal government as needing major repairs or unfit for human use.[34] While New Deal programs provided some benefits, especially in the larger cities, wage discrimination on WPA and other projects—coupled with general anti–New Deal resistance on the part of the state political establishment, which delayed the implementation of such programs as Social Security—limited the impact for black Virginia. If, as one historian of the Virginia New Deal has concluded, "the Virginia of 1939 was remarkably similar to that of ten years earlier," then that similarity had especially negative implications for African Americans.[35] Marginal political status reinforced marginal eco-nomic status. The poll tax and other mechanisms of disenfranchisement left the black quarter of Virginia's population with, as one contemporary commentator noted, "no effective voice in the formulation and administration of the laws under which [these residents] live."[36]

But to confront black Virginia in 1938 was also to confront the myriad mediating structures through which individual and group identities were shaped in the face of racism and poverty. Varied worlds of consciousness merited exploration, from the staid classrooms and chapels of Hampton Institute to the participation of a small but increasing number of black activists in the Congress of Industrial Organizations (CIO), the National Negro Congress, and other organizations, and to the cultures of survival that had developed on street corners and in alleys, fields, mills, and mines across the state. To confront black Virginia, in short, was to acknowledge the Jamesian proposition, so often denied by the Left and Right alike, that "profusion, not economy, may after all be reality's keynote."[37]

McNeill's visual production, amounting to no more than 160 images made with his Speed Graphic camera plus a couple of 35 mm rolls made with a borrowed Leica, certainly did not constitute a comprehensive rendering of Virginia's sociological complexity. What he did capture, however, was a notably more diverse black experience, a more profuse reality, than what the official assignment called for. McNeill documented workers on the job—those involved in menial sectors of the industrial and agricultural economy, and those in more skilled categories—as well as those without work. He recorded people making the most of petty authority, those wielding more genuine financial and intellectual authority, and residents of alley slums, of modest working-class neighborhoods, and of a few more-prosperous districts. He photographed rural life that had not changed in more than half a century and rural life with modern adaptations; organized religious and social gatherings, and impromptu manifestations of community; high culture forms and the cultures of the everyday (Figs. 4.5–4.7). The young photographer's ability to push the boundaries of Writers' Project expectations becomes more evident when one examines particular coverages.

One of McNeill's first shoots, a mini-story on tobacco workers at Richmond's Michaux stemmery, provides a case in point (Figs. 4.8–4.10). In focusing on the hogshead rollers, McNeill chose a group whose economic status was especially precarious even in a notoriously low-wage industry. Such laborers tended to fall on the low end of the average hourly wage range of twenty-two to thirty-eight cents for Virginia black male tobacco workers, as reported by the Bureau of Labor Statistics at mid-decade. And they often fell lower. Three-fifths of the Richmond hogshead rollers surveyed in sociologist Charles Johnson's 1935 study for the National Recovery Administration reported having been on the relief rolls. Seldom mentioned specifically in the wage-scale agreements negotiated by the Tobacco Workers International Union during this period, workers of the sort depicted by McNeill would still have trailed badly amid the general tobacco-worker wage gains registered at decade's end and into the 1940s.[38]

All but invisible economically, hogshead rollers tended to be invisible in photographic terms as well. Most commercial as well as U.S. Department of Agriculture (USDA) renderings emphasized the scale of production rather than the individual laborer, generally showing impressive rows of hogsheads with black workers positioned statically on top of, within, or around the huge containers.[39] By contrast, McNeill placed the laborer, and the laborer's typical encounter with the subject of his work, quite literally front and center. McNeill tried two low-angle views of the rollers in action. Unsatisfied with a first shot in which the workers were largely obscured by the hogshead, the photographer persisted with a second view that brought the human exertion closer to the viewer's space, the two rollers set prominently against a single looming hogshead (Fig. 4.8).

The emphasis on process suggested confidence and technique, and it also suggested a measure of pain, the implications of which were later described by one labor historian.

> The hogsheads of tobacco that [the workers] lugged around, weighing over a thousand pounds each, moved painfully on grudging naked axles. Many of . . . the workers bore in silence the agony of ruptures and bad backs from this hauling. If a worker wasn't torn up stacking the barrels five and six high, he might suffer a broken limb when a poorly balanced hogshead came tumbling down.[40]

Balancing workmen and hogshead, McNeill's image also balanced an element of traditional portraiture with grittier realism, as the neatly adjusted caps and faint smiles conveyed laborer pride but also suggested photographic artifice.

McNeill could easily have limited the tobacco coverage to this energetic work image that more than fulfilled Lewis's stated need for activity-oriented illustrations. But perhaps most significant about the Michaux visit was the fact that McNeill explored not only the demands of the work process but the burden of nonwork for laborers employed on an irregular, piece-work basis (Figs. 4.9 and 4.10). "Tobacco workers—employed and unemployed," McNeill's brief but pointed caption noted. More numerous than McNeill shots of workers with hogsheads were his views of workers *without* hogsheads, standing and sitting on the edge of the warehouse, waiting for a supervisor to give them the chance, as McNeill put it later, "to make a meager living."[41] In a sequence that recalled the thematic and compositional elements of his earlier *Bronx Slave Market* series, as well as elements similar to the Shahn cotton-picker series published in *Flash!*, McNeill moved from large group to small group to individual work seeker.

Such sensitivity to the waiting dimension of 1930s working life also marked McNeill's coverage of longshoremen in Norfolk. The obvious angle here would have been the play of men, ropes, and cargoes captured in most commercial and USDA photographs of dock work. But instead, McNeill focused on the inactivity that, in Norfolk and most other ports, represented the central problem of the longshore occupation before, during, and for some years after the depression.

In the era of the "casual" port, longshoremen could never be certain when, how long, or even whether they would be working on any given day. As one observer described the consequences two decades before the depression:

> There is required at all times a great deal of hanging about awaiting the arrival of ships or freight. This is a matter not of minutes but of hours; sometimes of whole days. Longshoremen, except while at work, are not allowed on the piers. They cannot go to their homes for fear they will not be on hand when wanted. Consequently, they must stand on the sidewalks, in doorways, or on street corners.[42]

With longshore regulars often waiting alongside drifting workers seeking temporary employ, an oversupply of labor had long been a fact of life in the longshore industry. Depression conditions further swelled the ranks of hopefuls, reduced already marginal incomes to the point that, early in the 1930s, a Bureau of Labor Statistics report estimated "conservatively" that more than 50 percent of the nation's longshoremen were on relief rolls, and further heightened the arbitrary authority of the hiring bosses. "If [the boss] didn't like you," remembered one 1930s longshoreman, "he'd point and say, 'Look, if you don't shape up, there are 50 men out there waiting to take your job,' which was true."[43]

In another FSA-influenced mini-story, McNeill began with a distant shot of prospective workers lining a street corner near the docks (Fig. 4.11). Picturing multiple clusters of men, McNeill accented the size of the potential labor pool as well as the racial character of that pool, which for the Virginia longshore industry as a whole was more than 90 percent black during this period.[44] Appropriately enough, the lone white figure in this image, perhaps the owner of the tavern on the block or perhaps a hiring boss, is on the street but not of the street, set off from the rest by his superior attire and his casually distant pose. McNeill's inclusion of the tavern sign and window lends hauntingly mixed implications; the tavern might be seen as a place of potential relaxation, as a gathering point for a dreary daily ritual, as a reminder of the petty corruption that marked the hiring system. One of the keys to gaining employment, charged the International Longshoremen's Association in the mid 1930s, involved "hanging around the waterfront saloons waiting for a chance to 'treat' the hiring bosses."[45]

A second view moved in closer to a group of four seated in a doorway, the gloom of the building and the littered street beyond lending a sense of foreboding to the wait (Fig. 4.12). For a third view, McNeill turned to just one of the sitters, whose hard stare spoke of pride but also of impatience and resentment (Fig. 4.13). "The look says, 'What the hell are you doing photographing me,'" mused McNeill later. "And I think it says a lot more. That sense of waiting for something to happen . . . summed up a lot of what I saw in Virginia."[46]

McNeill ventured further from the official labor theme in his visits to several urban neighborhoods, including the notorious Richmond slum, in the shadow of the tobacco plants, known as "Sophie's Alley." That venture proved productive, despite an unreliable Leica and McNeill's fear, not irrational, that his racial status afforded no badge of security in the alley context.

> Most black neighborhoods I could sort of cruise, looking for picture possibilities without arousing as much suspicion as a white photographer might, because in a lot of these places people had memories of white [commercial] 'pony' photographers looking to make a fast buck off them. So my race helped, to a degree. . . . But with a place like Sophie's Alley, you didn't want to hang around long, no matter who you were. You might get rolled.[47]

The photographer nevertheless managed twenty-five shots in the alley, not only focusing on the obvious signs of blight that USHA cameramen were apt to record (for example, an outdoor privy with open door exposing the primitive facilities within) but also finding more inventive ways to convey modes of endurance in a crowded, neglected, makeshift environment. They included the depiction of pant legs dangling from a clothesline and plunging into the foreground in one frame; in another frame, pigeons flying out of hastily constructed cages and into the viewer's space; and in other frames, a young boy and a dog trading places at an outdoor tap, sole source of water for many residences.

McNeill also approached one alley subculture, that of card players, with an uncommon respectfulness. One view set an especially serious, meditative group, positioned around a makeshift card table in the foreground, against a seemingly endless stretch of alleyway in the background, with distant figures caught up in what appear to be equally distinct worlds of concentration (Fig. 4.14). With its sense of gravity, the image avoided the happy-go-lucky stereotypes associated with black gambling. And with its sense of space defined as much by the consciousness of the alley dwellers (contemplating their respective pursuits) as by physical forms, it avoided the assumption of an equivalence between hopelessly degraded conditions and hopelessly degraded identities that underlay the typical USHA investigations and the periodic *Richmond Times-Dispatch* slum exposés.[48] Card-playing culture may not have been what New Deal administrators or *The Negro in Virginia* editors had in mind when they conceived of black community; but McNeill, despite his own security concerns in Sophie's Alley, had a sharper feel for what a later scholar called the patterns that helped "mitigate . . . circumvent, and occasionally avoid the disasters that confronted [residents] daily, as well as providing meaning, form, substance, and pleasure for their lives."[49] As one recent chronicler of 1930s black grassroots political activity in urban Virginia conceded about the importance of other involvements: "Vice, games of chance, and religion . . . served as primary reference points for many. For these individuals, the most pressing issue was not home sphere development or workplace advancement, but survival."[50]

McNeill also visited a somewhat more prosperous working-class neighborhood of Richmond, where he encountered a group of young men admiring a colleague's recently purchased automobile. The very notion of young men spending their limited earnings on cars met classic reformist disapproval in *The Negro in Virginia* text.

> Automobile ownership is high among Virginia Negroes; factory workers, waiters, laundry workers, maids, school teachers, and many other Negroes in low wage groups can be seen driving their cars around city streets. . . . Former $2,000 cars purchased for $200 and furnished with extra horns, lights, and other ornaments, offer pathetic evidence of the desire of many to be "distinguished."[51]

But McNeill saw other possibilities, though his more approving photograph was no simple salute to individual triumph (Fig. 4.15). McNeill, who later remembered asking the men to hold their poses for the camera, obviously had the opportunity to restructure the scene in terms of black newspaper and studio photography. He might have focused principally on the owner's success, fashioning a Richmond version of James VanDerZee's famous Harlem view of an elegant couple and sleek automobile.[52] Instead, he chose to retain what, at least for a moment, was an impression of neighborhood participation in the acquisition; and the smirking young women in the background lend an unusually irreverent dimension to the dynamic communal mix.

When McNeill turned to the activities of blacks in positions other than laborer, the portrayal did not always end up as the straightforward tribute to black accomplishment that would have followed naturally from *The Negro in Virginia* project aims. For example, when photographing a black guard at a near-deserted railroad crossing outside Richmond, McNeill responded to the guard's hostile glare with a camera glare of his own (Fig. 4.16). Forced to remain at a distance, McNeill used that distance for a long-range perspective that highlighted the smallness of the guard's domain, meanwhile juxtaposing the man's challenging look in the guard post window with a prominent sign warning, "No Loafers Allowed." The result suggested the petty arrogance of the functionary whom McNeill would later call the "biggest loafer of them all."[53] Territorial possessiveness, the viewer was reminded, extended beyond southern whites. In the process, McNeill implicated at least one black employee in the steadfast resistance to outside photographers shown by the Virginia railroads. Despite Lewis's carefully worded entreaties, appealing to the "fine spirit of cooperation between employer and employee" on the rails, officials of the Norfolk and Western and other companies refused to allow any Writers' Project cameramen near the tracks.[54]

McNeill also provided a complex take on banking activities at the offices of the black-owned Hampton Building and Loan. Whereas the typical black newspaper approach favored images of busy tellers and their expectant customers, impressive portraits of executives at their desks, and overviews of modern facilities, McNeill chose a less adulatory stance. The photographer waited for a loan applicant to arrive and depicted his ensuing discussion with a loan officer. Viewed across the desk are the contrasting postures and contrasting clothing of visitor and official, with the pool of light in the middle of the desk underscoring both the importance of the discussion and the significance of the division. Rather than simply admiring the black executive's polished performance, the viewer is drawn into an implicit tension between distinct socioeconomic worlds. Such tension also emerged elsewhere in McNeill's bank coverage, which included an image of a teller and a female customer that was organized, pointedly, around the metal grill separating the respective communities (Fig. 4.17).

Though McNeill's most intriguing images came when he pushed beyond official assignment objectives, there were also instances in which he worked creatively within the terms of the "active labor" scenario. His coverage of "Dr. Cunningham," the octogenarian herb doctor in the mountains above Roanoke, offered a case in point. Alerted to Cunningham's reputation by a YMCA contact in Roanoke, McNeill accompanied his contact to the doctor's isolated abode, which, by all accounts, Cunningham had built himself more than a half-century before. The portrait of the herb doctor that emerged (Figs. 4.18 and 4.19) departed from the convention reflected in most photographs of former slaves collected for the FWP slave narrative volumes, in the photos published in the FWP's *Drums and Shadows*, in most commercial renderings of black old-timers, and even in most FSA views of the same. Usually subjects were shown seated on decrepit porches or standing next to ancient trees, peering suspiciously or perplexedly at a world that has left them with lined faces, gnarled hands, bent postures.[55] McNeill's coverage, by contrast, emphasized Cunningham acting on his world. Here was the old man sharpening an axe, splitting a log, leading an energetic tour of the premises. While symbols of the old certainly abound in this series, McNeill avoided the most obvious angle on the primitive, namely, the subject's herbal mysticism. McNeill remembered: "He was constantly talking, mumbling, philosophizing as he led us around . . . pointing out that the [axe-grinding] post had been three feet across when he was young; now it was just a nub. But what struck me the most about this old man was what he had built. He had made something out of nothing."[56]

If Cunningham cooperated eagerly with McNeill's project, such was not always the case with the photographer's potential black subjects. One did not have to be a railroad guard to resist the camera, as McNeill found out in his attempts to document crab pickers on the coast and string bean pickers inland. Though McNeill managed one effective view of uniformed shellfish workers and shellfish mounds in a crowded assemblage topped by naked light bulbs (Fig. 4.20), he desisted from further investigation.

> I could feel the resentment all over the room . . . if they were going to be photographed, they at least wanted to be photographed in their Sunday best. It was one of those occasions when people were not proud of what they were doing. Same with the string bean pickers. Remember, some of those people in the field may have escaped from the Deep South, maybe even from chain gangs; anyone who had an authoritative implement like a camera, they interpreted as someone connected with law enforcement. It didn't matter that I was a black photographer. They didn't want their picture taken by anyone. So I took a distant shot, [then] did a sort of 'gotcha!' with one guy kneeling on the ground, looking annoyed at me . . . and left.[57]

Comparison of McNeill's all too brief coverage of the string bean pickers (Fig. 4.21) with Jack Delano's FSA series, two years later, on migrant agricultural laborers in Virginia, Maryland, and North Carolina, suggests some of the possibilities left unexplored by McNeill. Delano initially encountered even stiffer resistance from the workers, some of whom evidently assumed that he was a military-draft agent.[58] But Delano persisted in his efforts to overcome the hostility and ultimately generated an extended series that followed the migrants from field to shack to highway, from positions of vulnerability (laborers at work on their knees or sleeping in abandoned boxcars) to situations more illustrative of control (migrants studying a road map or taking a moment on the Norfolk–Cape Charles ferry to write a letter home).[59] The notion that Delano, a white photographer, might have simply used racial intimidation to construct a middle-class narrative does not explain the complexity of his visual product. More important here is the practical consideration that while the FSA photographer felt no hesitation about devoting time and film to a multilayered story that might or might not prove useful to his sponsors, McNeill felt compelled to snap and run. As he recalled:

> There were a lot of story possibilities that occurred to me during the trip, and I can remember feeling disappointed when it was over because of the stories I didn't get. But I had to be extremely stingy with film, because I didn't know whether I could get any more. There was never much time for stories; I'd be due at the next location in a matter of hours. I was driving alone, and I had to worry about things like sleeping and eating and changing clothes, too.[60]

Where McNeill encountered the most obvious resistance from white authorities, in the coal town of Pocahontas, he adopted a narrower documentary approach. He passed up the problematical home and town contexts that FSA photographer Marion Post Wolcott explored in September 1938 across the border in West Virginia, and he focused exclusively on a few black miners performing relatively high-skilled, mechanized jobs in the "show mine" (Fig. 4.22).[61] That the particular individuals photographed by McNeill had ascended the job ladder has been confirmed by Pocahontas sources, but larger economic and racial realities pointed in the opposite direction. "A black man at the scales or the motor? Maybe one in a hundred," reflects Frank Wilson, a native and longtime black educator in the border region. "Blacks cut the coal by hand. If you made $5.60 a day, you were lucky. That's one of the reasons why you never saw black miners [pictured] in the local Bluefield paper. Ministers, teachers, athletes . . . never miners."[62]

Other omissions in the McNeill coverage bore directly on ideological pressures established at the outset of the assignment, and here again, the FSA comparison is illuminating. Aware of the reign of Jim Crow in Virginia, McNeill heeded Lewis's implicit warning to stay away from the subject. Though evidence of racial segregation was hardly an FSA priority, there were at least a few FSA images referring directly to segregation in most southern states. Arthur Rothstein provided a general hint of the old order in the Old Dominion, thanks to his view of a Confederate flag hanging outside a Winchester movie theater presenting *Gone with the Wind* on Lincoln's birthday. And when Russell Lee, responsible for a particularly gripping FSA view of segregated drinking fountains in Oklahoma, visited the Pocahontas area of Virginia in 1946 for the Coal Mines Administration, he made sure to photograph the miners' racially bifurcated pool hall facilities.[63] While McNeill's subjects were almost exclusively black, the FSA photographers who toured Virginia often touched on black-white interactions revealing important social and economic hierarchies. Witness John Vachon's court-day story from Rustburg, showing, first, a commanding white judge, backed by an eye of God symbol on the wall, with black petitioners inside the courtroom and, then, the same judge revealing an edgier assertiveness, without the "divine" legitimation, standing opposite a well-dressed black gentleman on the street.[64]

The theme of black political and economic resistance, upon which McNeill had touched in his work for *Flash!*, did not carry over to his Virginia documentation, which made no references to the important black role in the CIO and other organized labor activity in the Virginia tobacco, longshore, and coal industries, among others. Ironically, the Michaux tobacco plant that McNeill visited in Richmond had been the site of a highly publicized black stemmers' strike the preceding year; and the Virginia press, black and mainstream, contained numerous reports in September 1938 of black-led strikes at two of Richmond's other plants, Export Leaf Tobacco and I. N. Vaughan.[65]

It was not just strike activity that was missed here. It was the reflection of a creative cultural syncretism in such informal events as that described by a black Richmond tobacco organizer of this period.

I am giving a bingo party on . . . Wednesday night . . . to try to get out some of the colored workers at Liggett and Myers; I want to have some handbills or cards printed announcing same, to be distributed to these people. We have to combat with about 7 or 8 CIO men in this town, and due to their system of organizing (no initiation fee) we must offer certain classes some form of drawing card.[66]

Black organizing, too, did not figure in FSA's coverage of Virginia, though FSA photographers recorded manifestations not far away. Even as late as November 1942, when Stryker's photographic unit was part of a more restrictive war information bureaucracy, Gordon Parks felt sufficiently free to cover a mass meeting in Washington, D.C. The purpose of the meeting was to protest the poll tax, and Stryker felt sufficiently committed to documentary experimentation to allow the most suggestive of these negatives to be printed and placed in the permanent file.[67]

Perhaps the most striking of the McNeill omissions in Virginia involved the labor group that he knew so well from New York. Domestic workers, of whom more than 80 percent in Virginia were black, made no appearance at all in McNeill's visual survey.[68] While Parks received unmistakable encouragement from Stryker to pursue the day-in-the-life-of-a-charwoman idea that produced the Ella Watson series, McNeill had received no such encouragement from Lewis. For the latter, the domestics subject afforded few examples of economic progress, and it involved issues that were, quite literally, too close to the white home.

Further limitations emerged in the photo-editing phase, after McNeill's active involvement with *The Negro in Virginia* project had ended. Strategies for selection and deployment of photographs in the book came from Lewis and Richardson in Virginia, and from Brown and Alsberg in Washington, D.C. At least initially, McNeill's overall Virginia output drew a warm reception from the project officials. "I saw some of the pictures," Brown wrote Lewis in October 1938. "They're good O.K., in line with the book. McNeill swears by the book. He used the word electrifying."[69] As the editors negotiated first with Viking Press and later with the eventual publisher, Hastings House, they showed continuing commitment to the concept of a strongly pictorial book, but somewhat less interest in McNeill's pictorial contributions. Of the forty-seven photographs ultimately used in *The Negro in Virginia*, only eleven were McNeill's. A majority came from more conventional sources: WPA Information Division shots of black literacy classes, familiar black achievement shots from Scurlock and black newspapers, a few rather pedestrian labor views from white commercial sources, and, ironically, several Highton contributions.

While the selections from McNeill reflected something of the diversity of professions that he photographed, the editorial emphasis lay with those images that fit more neatly into an active-laborer, black role-model narrative, beginning with a view of Dr. Cunningham grinding an axe, used on the original edition's cover. Few of the more adventurous photos made the final cut. Instead of McNeill's loan applicant–loan officer encounter, the editors ran a black newspaper view of a crowded bank lobby. The employed hogshead rollers appeared in the book; their unemployed counterparts did not.[70]

Editorial reshapings obscured McNeill's juxtapositions. The creative use of a discarded Packard chassis on an alfalfa wagon had prompted McNeill to photograph the wagon, but in the book version, the chassis was entirely cropped out, leaving a more predictable view of bales and balers (Fig. 4.23). In the case of the one bleak view that did make the book, the closeup of the single longshoreman, the captioning—merely "laborer"—concealed McNeill's examination of the specific rituals of the longshore realm. The gravity of that image was softened by its placement next to a commercial photo (contributed by the Hampton Institute president Howe) showing—of all subjects—a smiling maid.[71] To understand the Negro, quipped one reviewer, seeming to accept this superficial rendering of the black domestic, "this book beats asking the maid."[72] Perhaps most curious was the fate of McNeill's Sophie's Alley card-player shot, published not in *The Negro in Virginia* but in the general Virginia guide, where it was all but lost amid a genteel tour of historic highways and byways.[73] Reflected McNeill:

The pictures they selected [for *The Negro in Virginia*] weren't necessarily the ones I would have picked, but that was out of my control. I already knew, from my experience with black newspaper editors, that sometimes a photograph would be picked just because the editor would see his relative in it. And you have to remember my age. I was excited just to see *anything* of mine published![74]

The conservative visual editing probably helped the book's critical success when it appeared in July 1940. *The Negro in Virginia* drew a favorable brief from the Book-of-the-Month Club and longer, equally positive reviews in journals black-edited and white-edited (from the *Pittsburgh Courier* to the *New York Times* and *New York Herald-Tribune*), liberal and conservative (from *Commonweal* to *American Mercury*), national and state (from the *Saturday Review of Literature* to the *Richmond Times-Dispatch*).[75]

Inasmuch as the book's photographic dimension drew only occasional, nonspecific references, an "interesting" here and a "varied and informative" there, the visual selections did not divert reviewers' attention from what virtually all considered the heart of the work. The nineteenth-century chapters, and especially the implications of the former-slave testimonies therein, gained the bulk of the press exposure. When reviewers did turn to the contemporary life chapters in which McNeill's photos appeared, excitement waned. "The half-lost history of the old past [represents] the best part of this book, superior to the adequate and intelligent but more familiar story of the Virginia Negro's present," observed Jonathan Daniels in the *Saturday Review*.[76]

Still, if the "forgotten plums of prowess and achievement," as the *Chicago Defender* described them, tended to be appreciated more in the early chapters, the overall sense of affirmation of black progress sought by the editors of *The Negro in Virginia* emerged in the reviews. "It is a tragic story, but there are hints of a happy ending," reported the *Newport News Daily Press*.[77] In that respect, official reception suited the needs of a Virginia black establishment seeking historical legitimation of its "race" leadership and a federal government looking to put the explosive controversies of the New Deal behind. By contrast, reviewers approaching the FSA–Richard Wright collaboration the following year, *Twelve Million Black Voices*, could not avoid the pictorial message that the burden of the past as well as the present, in the Deep South as well as the Upper South, was a burden capable of driving blacks out of the region altogether.[78]

McNeill's involvement with the Writers' Project did not mark the last time that his photographic sponsors' agenda prevented full exposure of his photographic achievements. His experience in September 1946 with the United Negro College Fund (UNCF) proved to be, if anything, more disappointing in publication terms. Taking a month off from his Washington, D.C., news photo service to do a UNCF assignment on life at southern black universities during the postwar adjustment, McNeill was given the technical resources that he lacked for the earlier Virginia work. He visited eleven campuses and generated nearly one thousand views, pursuing extended photo-stories, with detailed captions, that examined institutional continuity and change, social contrasts, and racial mythologies. But UNCF officials made virtually no use of the material. As it turned out, McNeill's view of Hampton students reading the latest issue of *Ebony* bespoke trends that would have negative ramifications for the photographer himself (Fig. 4.24).

> I think what the [UNCF] editors wanted was the slick, sugarcoated kind of pictures being featured in *Ebony*, alongside those uplifting success stories that seemed to me a little too brilliant for belief. I had more of the documentary approach in mind, showing that accommodations for the vets were not always ideal, getting into the communities and photographing conditions that hadn't changed. And I was also up against [territorial] resentments . . . I'm sure the publicity people at the colleges didn't want the UNCF using an outsider's stuff.[79]

McNeill's news service work in Washington, D.C., afforded few opportunities for *The Negro in Virginia*–style investigations. Through the late 1950s, 1960s, and 1970s, McNeill's work at the State Department, where he spent his longest government tenure, afforded none. There, McNeill worked under the veteran black photographer and administrator James "Steve" Wright, whose quiet attack on departmental racial traditions emphasized the even distribution of assignments for the members of his integrated staff and equal chances for professional advancement, rather than any significant change in photographic content.[80]

The explorations that McNeill made for the Writers' Project would be taken up in later decades by other government camera people, such as Russell Lee for the Coal Mines Administration after World War II, photographers for Vista, the Environmental Protection Agency's Documerica staff, and the Department of Housing and Urban Development in the 1960s and 1970s. McNeill, the consummate professional at the State Department, found a degree of fulfillment in his narrower endeavors. There was a part of him that had always wanted to be recognized as a photographer, not simply a black photographer of the black experience. But there was also a part recognizing, as McNeill acknowledged, a certain "loss" of photographic vision in the later years.[81] That vision had been on display in Virginia, questioning assumptions Left and Right, white and black—and generating, if not a sustained rebellion, at least moments of transcendence.

Notes

1. All three "New Deal memories" from Robert McNeill, interview by the author, January 10, 1993.

2. Gordon Parks, *Choice of Weapons* (1966; reprint, St. Paul: Minnesota Historical Society Press, 1986); and Gordon Parks, *Voices in the Mirror: An Autobiography* (New York: Doubleday, 1990). See also Parks, interview by Richard Doud, December 30, 1964, transcript at Archives of American Art, Washington, D.C. For recent criticism of Stryker and the FSA, see especially James Curtis, *Mind's Eye, Mind's Truth: FSA Photography Reconsidered* (Philadelphia: Temple University Press, 1989); Maren Stange, *Symbols of Ideal Life: Social Documentary Photography in America, 1890–1950* (New York: Cambridge University Press, 1989); Maurice Berger, *How Art Becomes History: Essays on Art, Society, and Culture in Post New Deal America* (New York: HarperCollins Publishers, 1992); Andrea Fisher, *Let Us Now Praise Famous Women: Women Photographers for the U.S. Government, 1935–1944* (New York: Pandora Press, 1987); Pete Daniel and Sally Stein, eds., *Official Images: New Deal Photography* (Washington, D.C.: Smithsonian Institution Press, 1987); and Sally Stein, *Marion Post Wolcott: FSA Photographs* (Carmel, Calif.: Friends of Photography, 1983).

3. Roscoe Lewis, ed., *The Negro in Virginia* (New York: Hastings House, 1940).

4. Wright's Public Works Administration photographs, in RG 69, Series PWA, Still Picture Branch, National Archives at College Park, Maryland; Wright's and MacDougall's contributions to FWA, in RG 162, Series G, FWA, WP, and PBA, National Archives; Smith's OWI work, in RG 208, Series NP, National Archives, and in Farm Security Administration/Office of War Information Collection, Lots 988, 1823, 1826, 1841, 1842, 1883, 1893, 1904, 1908, 1914, 1915, 1943, 1961, 1966, 2128, 2175, 2177, and 2213, Prints and Photographs Division, Library of Congress, Washington, D.C. (hereinafter FSA/OWI Collection); Joseph's OWI contributions, in RG 208, Series NP, National Archives; Pollard's FAP New York City photos, in RG 69, Series ANP, National Archives. See also discussion of Smith and the OWI context in Nicholas Natanson, "Robert McNeill and Black Government Photographers," *History of Photography* 19, no. 1 (spring 1995): pp. 26–30; and discussion of Wright, Smith, and Joseph in Nicholas Natanson, *The Black Image in the New Deal: The Politics of FSA Photography* (Knoxville: University of Tennessee Press, 1992). Valuable perspectives on Wright, Smith, Joseph, MacDougall, and Pollard also came from Wright, interview with Nicholas Natanson, August 19, 1990; McNeill, interview with Nicholas Natanson, June 26, 1989; and Alfred Palmer, interview with Nicholas Natanson, August 18, 1990.

5. Edward L. Ayers, "Conclusion: If All the South Were Virginia," in *The Edge of the South: Life in Nineteenth-Century Virginia*, ed. Edward L. Ayers and John C. Willis (Charlottesville: University Press of Virginia, 1991), p. 247. See also Ayers, *The Promise of the New South: Life after Reconstruction* (New York; Oxford University Press, 1992), pp. vii–x.

6. See "The Story of a Voyage to West Africa," *Chicago Sun*, April 11, 1943, *Parade* magazine section, pp. 11–13; Julia Peterkin and Doris Ulmann, *Roll, Jordan, Roll* (New York: Robert O. Ballou, 1933); Aaron Siskind photos, in Harlem Document Collection, Library of Congress; Oscar Jordan WPA photos, in RG 69, Series N, Box 55, National Archives; Erskine Caldwell and Margaret Bourke-White, *You Have Seen Their Faces* (1937; reprint, New York: Modern Age Books, 1995); USHA photos, in RG 196, Series HA, National Archives. For fuller exposition of representational types, see Natanson, *The Black Image in the New Deal*, pp. 16–48.

7. "Servants Receive $3.50 Weekly in Lynchburg," *Norfolk Journal-Guide*, September 24, 1938, p. 6.

8. Jewell Mazique, interview with Nicholas Natanson, February 25, 1992. See also Barbara Orbach and Nicholas Natanson, "The Mirror Image: Black Washington in World War II Era Federal Photography," *Washington History* 4, no. 1 (spring/summer 1992): pp. 5–25.

9. Robert McNeill, interview with Nicholas Natanson, January 10, 1993.

10. See, for example, McNeill photos for "After the Fight," *Flash!* 1, no. 18 (July 5, 1937): pp. 14–15, and for "National Negro Congress," *Flash!* 1, no. 34 (October 25, 1937): pp. 18–19.

11. The 1937 *Bronx Slave Market* negatives, and negatives for all the 1938 McNeill Virginia images cited in this essay, are in Robert McNeill's personal collection, Washington, D.C. For FSA photos reproduced in *Flash!* to which McNeill would have had immediate exposure, see "In the Fields of Cotton," *Flash!* 1, no. 29 (September 20, 1937): pp. 10–11; "Peonage—Blight of a Nation," *Flash!* 2, no. 2 (March 22, 1938): p. 5; and "Menace of the Nation—Sharecroppers," *Flash!* 2, no. 58 (May 17, 1938): pp. 22–23.

12. McNeill interview, January 10, 1993.

13. "The Servant Problem," *Fortune* 17, no. 3 (March 1938): pp. 81–120.

14. "Bronx Slave Market," *Flash!* 1, no. 50 (February 14, 1938): pp. 8–10.

15. In RG 69, Federal Writers' Project Entry 27, Reports and Miscellaneous Records Relating to Negro Studies, 1936–1940, National Archives, see: WPA press release, "America Learns of Negro from Books of Federal Writers' Project," March 16, 1939, Box 200, Negro Press Digest folder; Brown to Frances Kendrick, "Projected Books Concerning Negroes," January 3, 1939, and Brown report to Henry Alsberg, "Negro Publications," November 18, 1939, both in Box 201, Negro Books folder.

16. Sterling Brown, "The Negro in Washington," in Federal Writers' Project, *Washington: City and Capital* (Washington, D.C.: Government Printing Office, 1937), pp. 68–90. See also Illinois Federal Writers' Project, *Cavalcade of the American Negro* (Chicago: Diamond Jubilee Exposition, 1940). Among southern state guides, see, for example, *Virginia: A Guide to the Old Dominion* (1940; reprint, New York: Oxford University Press, 1941); *Mississippi: A Guide to the Magnolia State* (New York: Viking Press, 1938); *North Carolina: A Guide to the Old North State* (Chapel Hill: University of North Carolina Press, 1939); *Tennessee: A Guide to the State* (New York: Viking Press, 1939); *Kentucky: A Guide to the Bluegrass State* (New York: Harcourt, Brace, and Company, 1939); and *Maryland: A Guide to the Old Line State* (New York: Oxford University Press, 1940). See Brown's comments on black coverage in state and city guides, in Brown to Alsberg, "Negro Material," June 8, 1937, Box 200, Memos folder, and Brown to Alsberg, "Existing Conditions in the Office of Negro Affairs," November 1938, Box 201, Negro Books folder, both in Federal Writers' Project Entry 27, National Archives. See also discussion of state guide coverage of blacks in Gary W. McDonogh, ed., *The Florida Negro: A Federal Writers' Project Legacy* (Jackson: University Press of Mississippi, 1993), pp. vii–xxxv; and overview of Brown and Alsberg roles, in Jerre Mangione, *The Dream and the Deal: The Federal Writers' Project, 1935–1943* (Boston: Little, Brown, and Company, 1972).

17. Georgia Federal Writers' Project, *Drums and Shadows: Survival Studies among the Georgia Coastal Negroes* (1940; reprint, Westport, Conn.: Greenwood Press, 1986).

18. Richardson to Alsberg, November 27, 1937, in RG 69, Federal Writers' Project Entry 13, Editorial Correspondence, Box 52, Negro in Virginia folder, National Archives. See also discussion of Richardson role, in Charles Perdue, ed., *Weevils in the Wheat: Interviews with Virginia Ex-Slaves* (Charlottesville: University of Virginia Press, 1980), and Perdue, foreword to Roscoe Lewis, ed., *The Negro in Virginia* (1940; reprint, Winston-Salem: John F. Blair, 1994), vii–xviii.

19. See, for example, Lewis to Alsberg, July 1, 1937, in Roscoe Lewis Papers, Virginia Writers' Project box, Miscellaneous Administrative Papers folder, Hampton University Archives, Hampton, Virginia.

20. Mangione, *The Dream and the Deal*, pp. 289–326.

21. "Testimony Cited on WPA Book Bias," *New York Times*, November 27, 1938, p. 1. See also *New York Times* reports of Woodrum Committee hearings, especially May 2, 1939, p. 1, and June 7, 1939, p. 1.

22. Richardson to Howe, May 19 and September 14, 1938, in Lewis Papers, Virginia Writers' Project box,

Correspondence—General folder, Hampton University Archives. On efforts to arrange sponsorship, see, for example, Lewis to Alsberg, March 9 and April 6, 1938, ibid., Miscellaneous Administrative Papers folder.

23. Howe to Alsberg, September 16, 1936, in RG 69, Federal Writers' Project Entry 27, Box 201, Negro Books folder, National Archives. See also Howe to Albert Bushnell Hart, February 25, 1939, ibid. For further reflection of these sentiments, see "Federal Writers Dig into History of Race in Virginia, Pull Out Forgotten Plums of Prowess, Achievement," *Chicago Defender*, June 4, 1938, pp. 6–7.

24. Lewis, ed., *The Negro in Virginia*, (1940 ed.), p. 351.

25. See draft additions, "The Negro in Virginia," in Lewis Papers, Virginia Writers' Project box, folder 4.

26. Lewis to Charles West on baseball segregation, April 25, 1939; Lewis to A. G. Richardson on educational support, October 5, 1937; and Lewis to A. B. Mackey on city-by-city disenfranchisement, June 16, 1938. All in Lewis Papers, Virginia Writers' Project box, Miscellaneous Administrative Papers folder.

27. See, for example, Alsberg to Richardson, "Photographs for State Guide," July 1, 1938; Richardson to Alsberg, July 16, 1938; Alsberg to Richardson, July 21, 1938; and Richardson to Alsberg, July 22, 1938. All in RG 69, Federal Writers' Project Entry 13, Box 52, Negro in Virginia folder, National Archives.

28. *Virginia: A Guide to the Old Dominion*, porch sitter between pp. 562 and 563, and daffodil seller opposite p. 248. See also descriptions of church view and other Highton photos, in Charles Wood to Maurice Howe, August 11, 1938; Wood to William Pryor, August 16, 1938; and Alsberg to Richardson, August 16, 1938. All in RG 69, Federal Writers' Project Entry 13, Box 52, Negro in Virginia folder, National Archives.

29. Richardson to Alsberg, August 20, 1938, in RG 69, Federal Writers' Project Entry 13, Box 52, Negro in Virginia folder, National Archives.

30. Charles Wood to Maurice Howe, August 11, 1938, ibid. See also Howe to Wood, August 10, 1938, ibid.

31. "Photographer Named WPA Consultant," *Norfolk Journal-Guide*, September 24, 1938, p. 13. See also Wood to Clair Laning, August 17, 1938; and Myrtle Hawkins to Rives Lamb, August 26, 1938. Both in RG 69, Federal Writers' Project Entry 13, Box 52, Negro in Virginia folder, National Archives.

32. McNeill interview, January 10, 1993.

33. Ibid.

34. See Harry W. Roberts, "Disadvantaging Factors in the Life of Rural Virginia Negroes," *Virginia State College Gazette* 1, no. 1 (February 1945): pp. 11–12; and Richard Sterner, *The Negro's Share: A Study of Income, Consumption, Housing, and Public Assistance* (1943; reprint, Westport, Conn.: Greenwood Press, 1971), pp. 371–73, 404.

35. Ronald L. Heinemann, *Depression and New Deal in Virginia: The Enduring Dominion* (Charlottesville: University Press of Virginia, 1983), p. 172.

36. Robert E. Martin, *Negro Disenfranchisement in Virginia* (Washington, D.C.: Howard University Press, 1938), p. 159.

37. Bruce Kuklick, ed., *William James: Writings, 1902–1910* (New York: Library of America, 1987), p. 570.

38. For Bureau of Labor Statistics studies, see Mortier W. La Fever, "Wages and Hours of Labor: Earnings in Cigarette, Snuff, and Chewing and Smoking Tobacco Plants, 1933–35," *Monthly Labor Review* 25 (May 1936): pp. 1322–35; and Jacob Perlman, "The Negro in Industry: Earnings and Hours of Negro Workers in Independent Tobacco Stemmeries in 1933 and 1935," *Monthly Labor Review* 26 (May 1937): pp. 1153–72. For Charles Johnson's study, see tobacco workers survey records from Richmond, included in RG 9, Entry 289, Records of the Division of Review—Industries Studies Section, Records of the Tobacco Unit, Box 1, Tobacco Workers folder, National Archives. For wage-scale agreements, see, for example, Tobacco Workers International Union Papers, Series 3, Box 12 (Locals 182, 183, and 192, 1937–1940 agree-

ments) and Box 26 (Locals 203, 214, and 215, 1937–1944 agreements), University of Maryland Archives, College Park.

39. See, for example, tobacco processing photos in RG 16, Series G, Box 295; RG 151, Series FC, Box 99; and RG 83, Series ML, Box 31. All in National Archives. See also the Virginia commercial tobacco files in George Cook Collection, Prints and Photographs Division, Valentine Museum of the Life and History of Richmond, Virginia; and tobacco entries in Still Images Collection, George Meany Memorial Archives, Silver Spring, Maryland.

40. Stuart Bruce Kaufman, *Challenge and Change: The History of the Tobacco Workers International Union* (Urbana: University of Illinois Press, 1986), p. 68.

41. McNeill interview, January 10, 1993.

42. Charles B. Barnes, *The Longshoremen* (New York: Russell Sage Foundation, 1915), p. 50. For more typical views of longshoremen, see RG 16, Series G, Boxes 100–104, National Archives; and longshoremen entries in Still Images Collection, Meany Memorial Archives.

43. For the Bureau of Labor Statistics study, see Boris Stern, "Employment Conditions and Unemployment Relief: Longshore Labor Conditions and Port Decasualization in the United States," *Monthly Labor Review* 22 (December 1933): pp. 1299–1306. Longshoreman Germain Bulcke quoted in Howard Kimeldorf, "Sources of Working-Class Insurgency: Politics and Longshore Unionism during the 1930s," in *Insurgent Workers: Studies of the Origins of Industrial Unionism on the East and West Coast Docks and in the South during the 1930s*, ed. Maurice Zeitlin (Los Angeles: Institute of Industrial Relations, University of California, Los Angeles, 1987), p. 11. Other later descriptions of the "shape up" are in Lester Rubin, *Racial Policies of American Industry, Report No. 29: The Negro Longshore Industry* (Philadelphia: University of Pennsylvania Press, 1974), p. 24; Bruce Nelson, *Workers on the Waterfront: Seamen, Longshoremen, and Unionism in the 1930s* (Urbana: University of Illinois Press, 1988), pp. 105, 106, 162; and David Wellman, *The Union Makes Us Strong: Radical Unionism on the San Francisco Waterfront* (New York: Cambridge University Press, 1995), p. 60.

44. Rubin, *Racial Policies of American Industry, Report No. 29*, p. 88.

45. International Longshoremen's Association Local 38-79 publication, "The Truth about the Waterfront," 1935, quoted in Nelson, *Workers on the Waterfront*, p. 162.

46. McNeill interview, January 10, 1993.

47. Ibid.

48. Gordon Parks's Washington, D.C., slum coverage is in FSA/OWI Collection, Lot 160. Typical USHA slum coverage is represented by Richard Oliver's "Slum Dwelling, Before Clearance," Macon, Georgia, 1940, in RG 196, Series HA, Box 2, National Archives; and "Human Misery in Slum Area Presents Problem to Richmond," *Richmond Times-Dispatch*, January 15, 1939, sec. 4, pp. 1–2.

49. James Borchert, *Alley Life in Washington* (Urbana: University of Illinois Press, 1982), p. 223.

50. Earl Lewis, *In Their Own Interests: Race, Class, and Power in Twentieth-Century Norfolk, Virginia* (Berkeley and Los Angeles: University of California Press, 1991), p. 152.

51. Lewis, ed., *The Negro in Virginia*, p. 350.

52. For discussion of the VanDerZee image, see Natanson, *The Black Image in the New Deal*, pp. 30–31.

53. McNeill interview, June 26, 1989.

54. Lewis to Norfolk and Western Railway Company, April 7, 1938, Lewis Papers, Virginia Writers' Project box, Miscellaneous Administrative Papers folder.

55. FWP Slave Narratives (volumes with photographic illustrations), in Boxes 918–932, Manuscript Division, Library of Congress, especially the visual entries in the volumes for Arkansas, Georgia, North Carolina, South Carolina, and Texas

(Virginia volume contains no photographs); Muriel Barrow Bell and Malcolm Bell photos, in Georgia Federal Writers' Project, *Drums and Shadows*, plates 5, 7, 8, 13, 14, 15, 17, 19, 23, and 24; commercial views of former slaves gathered for *The Negro in Virginia* project files, in Lewis Papers, Virginia Writers' Project box, Correspondence—General folder. For FSA example, see Dorothea Lange views of former slaves on steps of Greene County, Georgia, mansion, in FSA/OWI Collection, Lot 1545.

56. McNeill interview, January 10, 1993.

57. Ibid.

58. Delano to Stryker, July 2, 1940, Roy E. Stryker Papers, microfilm reel NDA 25, Archives of American Art.

59. Delano coverage of migrant workers in FSA/OWI Collection, Lots 1384, 1440, 1441, 1522. On Virginia work of Delano and other FSA photographers, see also Brooks Johnson, ed., *Mountaineers to Main Streets: The Old Dominion as Seen through the FSA Photographs* (Norfolk: Chrysler Museum, 1985).

60. McNeill interview, January 10, 1993.

61. In FSA/OWI Collection: Wolcott coverage of West Virginia coal miners, Lots 1730–1734, and Shahn's 1935 mining coverages from West Virginia, Lots 1721–1722.

62. Background on particular miners photographed by McNeill—Emmett Bryant and John Muse—provided by former Pocahontas resident Herman Branson, conversation with the author, April 15, 1993; memories of border region from Frank Wilson, conversation with the author, July 20, 1993. See also Frank Wilson, "Memories of Bluestone High," *Bramwell (West Virginia) Aristocrat*, February 1993, and regional history project interview with Pocahontas resident Julia Wilkins, included in holdings of Eastern Regional Coal Archives, Craft Memorial Library, Bluefield, West Virginia. For historians' accounts of race-profession nexus, see especially Price V. Fishback, *Soft Coal, Hard Choices: The Economic Welfare of Bituminous Coal Miners, 1890–1930* (New York: Oxford University Press, 1992), pp. 171–92; Ronald L. Lewis, *Black Coal Miners in America: Race, Class, and Community Conflict, 1780–1980* (Lexington: University Press of Kentucky, 1986), pp. 167–82; and Crandall A. Shifflett, *Coal Towns: Life, Work, and Culture in Company Towns of Southern Appalachia, 1880–1960* (Knoxville: University of Tennessee Press, 1991).

63. Lee's Virginia coal mining photos for Medical Survey of the Bituminous Coal Industry, in RG 245, Series MS, Box 3, National Archives; Lee's earlier view of Oklahoma segregation sign, in FSA/OWI Collection, Lot 540; Rothstein's Winchester theater image, in FSA/Collection, Lot 1437.

64. Vachon's Rustburg coverage, in FSA/OWI Collection, Lot 1438.

65. See accounts of Michaux strike in *Richmond Times-Dispatch*, April 20, 1937, p. 1; April 24, p. 3; April 28, p. 3; and April 29, p. 13; accounts of Export Leaf Tobacco strike in *Norfolk Journal-Guide*, August 27, 1938, sec. 2, p. 1; September 10, sec. 2, p. 11; accounts of Vaughan strike in *Norfolk Journal-Guide*, October 8, 1938, sec. 2, p. 11; October 24, sec. 2, p. 11; and in *Richmond Times-Dispatch*, September 28, 1938, p. 12; September 29, p. 12; and September 30, p. 12. See also Kaufman, *Challenge and Change*, pp. 94–95.

66. C. H. Farmer to Samuel Evans, May 18, 1937, Tobacco Workers International Union Papers, Series 2, Box 21, Farmer folder, University of Maryland Archives.

67. Parks's coverage of Washington, D.C., mass meeting, in FSA/OWI Collection, Lot 269. Careful comparison of printed and unprinted negatives from this series does not reveal any pattern of Stryker censorship. For discussion of printed versus unprinted negatives in other politically sensitive FSA series relating to blacks, see Natanson, *The Black Image in the New Deal*, pp. 81–82.

68. Depression-era statistics on domestic workers, in Roberts, "Disadvantaging Factors," pp. 9–10.

69. Brown to Lewis, October 11, 1938, in Lewis Papers, Virginia Writers' Project box, General Correspondence folder.

70. For negotiations with publishers, see, for example, Howe to Marshall Best, November 30, 1939, in Arthur Howe Papers, Box 23, Virginia Federal Writers' Project—1939 folder, Hampton University Archives; for final selections, see Lewis, ed., *The Negro in Virginia*, cover and between pp. 316 and 317 (Dr. Cunningham), p. 117 (bank depositors), between pp. 316 and 317 (hogshead rollers).

71. Lewis, ed., *The Negro in Virginia*, between pp. 316 and 317 (pitching alfalfa, laborer, housemaid).

72. Book review, *Baltimore Sun*, July 21, 1940, excerpted in Lewis Papers, Virginia Writers' Project box, folder 3.

73. *Virginia: A Guide to the Old Dominion*, opposite p. 563.

74. McNeill interview, January 10, 1993.

75. On submission of maid photo, see Richardson to Howe, April 2, 1940, Howe Papers, Box 23, Virginia Federal Writers' Project—1940 folder; for reception, see "Good WPA Book on the Negro," *Book of the Month Club News*, September 1940, reproduced in review compilation, Lewis Papers, Virginia Writers' Project box, folder 3; "The Negro Workers of Virginia," *New York Times*, August 11, 1940, sec. 6, p. 11; George S. Schuyler, "In Ole Virginny," *Pittsburgh Courier*, September 28, 1940, p. 7; "The Negro in Virginia," *Commonweal*, September 27, 1940, p. 475; Jonathan Daniels, "History of the Negro," *Saturday Review of Literature*, September 7, 1940, p. 15; "The Negro in Virginia," *American Mercury*, September 1940, p. 118; Martin Singer, "The Negro as He Is in Virginia," *Richmond Times-Dispatch*, July 14, 1940, sec. 4, p. 7; Beatrice M. Murphy, "The Negro in Virginia," *Baltimore Afro-American*, October 12, 1940, p. 24; Roi Ottley, "Studying the Old South," *New York Herald-Tribune*, January 19, 1941, sec. 9, p. 14.

76. Passing photo references, in "The Negro in Virginia," *Commonweal*, September 27, 1940, p. 475; *New York Times*, August 11, 1940, sec. 6, p. 11; Daniels, "History of the Negro," p. 15. See also Ottley remarks on contemporary life chapters, in Ottley, "Studying the Old South," sec. 9, p. 14.

77. "Federal Writers Dig into History of Race in Virginia; Pull Out Forgotten Plums of Prowess, Achievement," *Chicago Defender*, June 4, 1938, pp. 6–7; review, *Newport News Daily Press*, August 7, 1940, excerpted in review compilation, Lewis Papers, Virginia Writers' Project box, folder 3.

78. See, for example, William Shands Meacham, "The Bitter Saga of the Negro: The Drama of Centuries Compressed into a Short Book Written in Astringent Prose," *New York Times*, November 23, 1941, sec. 6, p. 11; Richard Crandell, "Dark Thoughts on Dark Citizens," *New York Herald-Tribune*, November 23, 1941, sec. 9, p. 8; and J. A. Schuyler, "12 Million Black Voices," *Pittsburgh Courier*, December 6, 1941, p. 7. For extended analysis of reviewer reception of *Twelve Million Black Voices*, see Natanson, *The Black Image in the New Deal*, pp. 251–55.

79. McNeill interview, January 10, 1993. Contact prints of McNeill's UNCF images are in McNeill's personal collection; original negatives are at Schomburg Center for Research in Black Culture.

80. James Stephen Wright, interview with Nicholas Natanson, August 19, 1990.

81. McNeill interview, January 10, 1993. In National Archives: Lee's work for Coal Mines Administration, in RG 245, Series MS; Documerica photography in RG 412, Series DA; Vista photography in RG 362, Series VS; Housing and Urban Development Photo Library, RG 207, Series N.

4.1 Oscar Jordan, *Mattress Making*, 1936, Savannah, Georgia. Works Progress Administration files, RG 69, Series N, Box 55, Negative 1393, National Archives.

4.2 Robert H. McNeill, from *Bronx Slave Market* series, 1937, New York City. Courtesy of Robert H. McNeill, Washington, D.C.

4.3 Robert H. McNeill, from *Bronx Slave Market* series, 1937, New York City. Courtesy of Robert H. McNeill, Washington, D.C.

4.4 Robert H. McNeill, from *Bronx Slave Market* series, 1937, New York City. Courtesy of Robert H. McNeill, Washington, D.C.

4.5 Robert H. McNeill, from *Sandlot Football* series, 1938, Norfolk, Virginia. Courtesy of Robert H. McNeill, Washington, D.C.

4.6 Robert H. McNeill, from *Sandlot Football* series, 1938, Norfolk, Virginia. Courtesy of Robert H. McNeill, Washington, D.C.

4.7 Robert H. McNeill. *Country Store,* 1938, outside Hampton, Virginia. Courtesy of Robert H. McNeill, Washington, D.C.

4.8 Robert H. McNeill, *Tobacco Workers Rolling Hogshea*d, 1938, Richmond, Virginia. Courtesy of Robert H. McNeill, Washington, D.C.

4.9 Robert H. McNeill, from *Tobacco Workers—Employed and Unemployed* series, 1938, Richmond, Virginia. Courtesy of Robert H. McNeill, Washington, D.C.

4.10 Robert H. McNeill, from *Tobacco Workers—Employed and Unemployed* series, 1938, Richmond, Virginia. Courtesy of Robert H. McNeill, Washington, D.C.

4.11 Robert H. McNeill, from *Longshoremen* series, 1938, Norfolk, Virginia. Courtesy of Robert H. McNeill, Washington, D.C.

4.12 Robert H. McNeill, from *Longshoremen* series, 1938, Norfolk, Virginia. Courtesy of Robert H. McNeill, Washington, D.C.

4.13 Robert H. McNeill, from *Longshoremen* series, 1938, Norfolk, Virginia. Courtesy of Robert H. McNeill, Washington, D.C.

4.14 Robert H. McNeill, from *Sophie's Alley* series, 1938, Richmond, Virginia. Courtesy of Robert H. McNeill, Washington, D.C.

4.15 Robert H. McNeill, *New Car*, 1938, Richmond, Virginia. Courtesy of Robert H. McNeill, Washington, D.C.

4.16 Robert H. McNeill, *Railroad Crossing*, 1938, Richmond, Virginia. Courtesy of Robert H. McNeill, Washington, D.C.

4.17 Robert H. McNeill, from *Hampton Building and Loan* series, 1938, Hampton, Virginia. Courtesy of Robert H. McNeill, Washington, D.C.

4.18 Robert H. McNeill, from *Dr. Cunningham* series, 1938, outside Roanoke, Virginia. Courtesy of Robert H. McNeill, Washington, D.C.

4.19 Robert H. McNeill, from *Dr. Cunningham* series, 1938, outside Roanoke, Virginia. Courtesy of Robert H. McNeill, Washington, D.C.

4.20 Robert H. McNeill, *Crab Pickers*, 1938, outside Hampton, Virginia. Courtesy of Robert H. McNeill, Washington, D.C.

4.21 Robert H. McNeill, from *String Bean Pickers* series, 1938, south central Virginia. Courtesy of Robert H. McNeill, Washington, D.C.

4.22 Robert H. McNeill, from *Coal Miners, Pocahontas* series, 1938, Virginia. Courtesy of Robert H. McNeill, Washington, D.C.

4.23 Robert H. McNeill, from *Alfalfa* series, 1938, outside Williamsburg, Virginia. Courtesy of Robert H. McNeill, Washington, D.C.

4.24 Robert H. McNeill, from *United Negro College Fund Survey*, 1946, Hampton, Virginia. Courtesy of Robert H. McNeill, Washington, D.C.

5. THE SCURLOCK STUDIO

Jane Freundel Levey

Everybody knew the Scurlock family. You always saw the Scurlocks making photographs. . . .
The father had an air of importance—he knew what he was and what he could do. And Bobby
took after his father.

—Ellsworth Davis, Washington Post photographer.

For nearly a century the Scurlock family photographed Washington's African American community, creating art as well as a rich historical resource. Addison N. Scurlock began working as a professional photographer in 1904 and established the Scurlock Studio at Ninth and U Streets NW in 1911. The business would later expand to include studios at 1623 and 1803 Connecticut Avenue and a color laboratory at 1813 Eighteenth Street. In the 1930s, Addison was joined in the photography business by his sons, George H. and Robert S., and Robert continued to operate the family business until his death in 1994.[1]

Recognized for their artistic qualities by numerous art galleries—the Corcoran Gallery of Art mounted studio founder Addison Scurlock's first one-man exhibit in 1976—the Scurlock photographs, represented by the images following this essay, constitute an unusually rich source for the historian of Washington, D.C., particularly of its black community. The historian's immediate context for understanding the Scurlock pictures is a commercial one. First, many of the studio's earliest subjects appear in Scurlock photographs because the studio's patrons could afford to commission their portraits. Second, many of the later photographs were produced to meet the demands of the national press and to reflect the documentary style and attempted objectivity of the journalist. In addition, the work of the Scurlock family, which spans photographic history from the time of the old, clumsy view cameras to the lightning-fast 35 mm cameras of today, offers a survey of the range of creative photographic technique.[2]

Addison Scurlock was born on June 19, 1883, in Fayetteville, North Carolina. His father, George Clay Scurlock, was a politician who ran unsuccessfully for the North Carolina Senate. In 1900, after Addison had graduated from high school, the family moved to Washington, D.C., where George Clay Scurlock worked as a messenger for the U.S. Treasury Department to support his family while he read law. Once he passed the bar examination, he opened a law office in the 1100 block of U Street.[3]

Young Addison Scurlock had already decided to pursue photography when the family arrived in Washington. From 1900 until 1904 he studied portrait photography as an apprentice to prominent photographer Moses P. Rice, who had studios on Pennsylvania Avenue. There Scurlock learned the basics of photographic portraiture, using large view cameras mounted on tripods and relying on natural light or the use of highly explosive flash powder. He also learned the entire range of laboratory work, including mixing his own solutions, retouching negatives, and creating tints and borders.[4]

In 1904, Scurlock began his own photographic operations, accepting clients at his parents' home in the 500 block of Florida Avenue NW and photographing students at Howard University, at the M Street and Armstrong High Schools, and at black universities and high schools around the South.[5] In 1911, he opened the Scurlock Studio at 900 U Street, concentrating on portraiture and general photography.[6]

The Washington, D.C., that Addison Scurlock began to photograph had a large black community (one-third of the total population) with strong institutions and long traditions.[7] This black community counted many generations of residence in the capital area and ancestors who had lived as free people in the years before the Civil War. While the dominant spirit of the city was that of the segregated South, and segregated schools, hospitals, and institutions prevailed, turn-of-the-century Washington offered black Americans the economic and social opportunities of urban life. As historian Michael Winston pointed out in his introduction to the Corcoran Gallery's 1976 Scurlock exhibition catalog:

Despite the serious limitations of segregation, Washington attracted an unusual black population. Its colored public schools were known throughout the nation as highly competitive and the best available to Negroes. . . . The agencies of the Federal Government, though riddled with discrimination, offered stable employment. . . . Some intellectual and cultural organizations played a significant role in making Washington a cultural capital . . . the Bethel Literary and Historical Association, founded in 1881; the American Negro Academy (1897); the Coleridge-Taylor Choral Society (1901); and the Association for the Study of Negro Life and History (1915). The most important institution in this regard, of course, was Howard University (1867) . . . [which] trained nearly half of the nation's black physicians and dentists and more than 90 percent of all the black lawyers.[8]

By the time Addison Scurlock opened his studio, Washington could claim an African American community of remarkable cultural and intellectual vibrancy. Its middle class clustered in the near northwest neighborhoods now known as Shaw and LeDroit Park, where most of the black community's churches, schools, and businesses, including the Scurlock Studio, were located. Many referred to U Street as the black Connecticut Avenue. The studio found clients among this society's leaders, brides, graduates, achievers, and visitors.[9] The portrait studio concentrated on black customers first. "Dad didn't restrict his work because of his race," recalled Robert Scurlock. "He operated in the neighborhood—and cut quite a figure there." Within a decade, Addison Scurlock had acquired a national reputation.[10]

The Scurlock Studio not only photographed important black Washingtonians—and many white ones—but often received invitations to record the Washington visits of prominent black Americans. As the official photographer of Howard University from the early 1900s until Addison Scurlock's death in 1964, the studio recorded all aspects of university life. A master of the panorama camera, which produces a particularly finely focused image of very large groups, Scurlock was a fixture on the local convention and banquet scene and well known in the community at large.[11]

In a 1976 *Washington Post* feature, journalist Jacqueline Trescott described Scurlock's perfectionism.

He was an easy-going man, very serious, rare to pursue an argument or raise his leisurely voice. . . . He was consumed with doing everything well. Once, while photographing the Dunbar [High School] Cadet Corps on the White House lawn with President Calvin Coolidge, he boldly walked up to Coolidge, much to the consternation of the Secret Service, and moved the President around. He demanded the same persistence from his employees and they returned a staunch loyalty.[12]

Addison Scurlock produced a series of portraits of black leaders that historian Carter G. Woodson distributed to black schools nationwide. He photographed sororities and social clubs, cotillions, business interiors, and weddings.[13] But his portraiture remained the studio's calling card. "For years one of the marks of arriving socially in black Washington was to have your portrait hanging in Scurlock's window," according to Trescott's article.[14]

Addison Scurlock and his wife, Mamie, lived at 1202 T Street NW, just a few blocks from the studio.[15] Mamie worked as the studio's business manager, and their sons, Robert and George, grew up in a comfortable, middle-class style. While they were expected to run errands or help in the darkroom, the boys were also free to pursue sports and other favorite leisure activities. "We had plenty of everything," recalled Robert. The community that was apparently so cohesive under segregation had the resources in some ways to protect its offspring from the harshness of segregation. "There were parties and other activities. Our social life was spent apart from the city as a whole, but nothing about it was unpleasant. . . . We never felt the apparent dissatisfaction with life that became apparent in the 1950s and 1960s. Of course plenty of people were aware they were being discriminated against." Indeed, the U Street of Robert Scurlock's youth offered a respite from the sharply divided city. The Howard Theater, a renowned stop on the vaudeville circuit, regularly attracted white customers for its stage shows and, later, jazz concerts. "Those were whites," recalled Robert Scurlock with more than a little irony, "who understood that the black on our hands wouldn't rub off."[16]

After graduating from Howard University, Robert and then George joined the family business, which had begun supplying news photos to the black press, both nationally and locally. Among their clients were the Washington-based *Tribune* and *Afro-American* (capital edition), and the *Norfolk Journal-Guide, Pittsburgh Courier, Cleveland Call and Post,* and *New York Amsterdam News.* The demands of photojournalism especially appealed to Robert, who produced much of the spot news commissioned by client newspapers and occasionally covered events for their potential historic value.[17]

The Scurlock brothers had learned the careful techniques of their father, including retouching and hand bordering. By the early 1940s, they were integral members of the studio. Robert left the family enterprise for four years to serve in the Army Air Force in World War II under Benjamin O. Davis Jr. He explored Europe with his camera, focusing especially on daily life in the Italian countryside. Fortunately for Addison, then in his sixties, George did not pass the army physical. He took over the nonportrait work during the war, allowing Addison to concentrate on his specialty. At the war's end, Robert came home to rejoin the family business.[18]

From 1948 until 1952, Robert and George operated the Capital School of Photography, where numerous, young former soldiers such as Ellsworth Davis, a future *Washington Post* photographer, and Bernie Boston of the *Los Angeles Times* studied under the GI Bill.[19] Among other students was a very young Jacqueline Bouvier, who was sent there by the *Washington Times-Herald* to learn enough photography to become the newspaper's inquiring photographer. She met Senator John F. Kennedy while on assignment.[20]

With the opening of Custom Craft Studios in 1952, Robert Scurlock became a pioneer in the processing of color photography, and a color photographer whose work was commissioned not only by local clients such as the U.S. State and Commerce Departments but also by such national magazines as *Ebony, Our World, Life*, and *Look*.[21] Robert's color work attracted the attention of scholars of history and photography. His color photographs of upper Fourteenth Street during the riots that followed the 1968 assassination of Martin Luther King Jr., for example, were published in *Life* magazine and continue to turn up in a variety of publications.[22]

The Scurlock studios on Connecticut Avenue closed in the early 1970s; the Ninth Street studio was demolished in 1983 to make way for the Metro subway system. Robert Scurlock continued to operate the business out of the one remaining studio, Custom Craft, until his death in 1994. There, his color portraits of clients such as Effi Barry, former wife of Mayor Marion Barry, and statesman and educator Ralph Bunche, and pictures of the façades of local banks were displayed alongside a few sepia-toned portraits from the early days. A complete catalog of the Scurlock oeuvre remains to be written; the consolidation and organization of the collection has yet to be attempted. But the files of the Scurlock archive hold portraits of such notable subjects as educator Mary Church Terrell, composer Samuel Coleridge-Taylor, engineer Archie Alexander, intellectual and political leader W. E. B. Du Bois, former first lady Mamie Eisenhower, singer Billy Eckstine, physician and researcher Charles R. Drew, opera singer Madame Lillian Evanti, historian John Hope Franklin, and poet Sterling Brown, among many, many others. There are interiors of businesses, views of children at play, scenes of riot and peace.[23] They were all made "in the course of business," yet they stand today as history not only of this city but of a highly self-sufficient black community scarcely noted at the time by the majority of white Washingtonians.[24]

The Scurlock photographs reflect a great span of time and variety of subjects. Because records are inexact and the studio employed nonfamily photographers over its long history, it is not always possible to know who actually made a particular picture. There is, however, a Scurlock "look," a very high technical quality in which light plays evenly and attractively across the features of the subjects. The portraits are carefully retouched to mask eye circles or crow's feet and to create even-textured complexions. There is a remarkably clear focus to every face in the group pictures. Perhaps the most distinctive hallmark of the Scurlock photograph is the dignity, the uplifting quality, of the demeanor of every subject, captured by photographers who clearly saw each one as above the ordinary.

Notes

This essay is adapted from Jane Freundel Levey, "The Scurlock Studio," *Washington History: Magazine of The Historical Society of Washington, D.C.* 1, no. 1 (Spring 1989). Used with permission.

1. Robert S. Scurlock, interview by the author, January 6, 1989, Washington, D.C.

2. *The Historic Photographs of Addison N. Scurlock*, exhibition catalog (Washington, D.C.: Corcoran Gallery of Art, 1976); Robert S. Scurlock, interviews by the author, January 24 and February 22, 1989. Scurlock photographs were also exhibited in the "Scurlock Family Photographers" show at Chicago's Black Women's Collaborative in 1981, and in "A Century of Black Photographers," a traveling exhibit of the Rhode Island School of Design Museum of Art in 1983.

3. Jacqueline Trescott, "Love of the People, Control of the Craft," *Washington Post*, June 13, 1976.

4. *The Historic Photographs of Addison N. Scurlock*; Scurlock interview, January 24, 1989.

5. Trescott, "Love of the People, Control of the Craft,"; Scurlock interview, January 24, 1989.

6. Scurlock interview, January 6, 1989.

7. Constance McLaughlin Green, *The Secret City: A History of Race Relations in the Nation's Capital* (Princeton, N.J.: Princeton University Press, 1967), 200.

8. Michael R. Winston, "Introduction to Washington and the 'Secret City,'" in *The Historic Photographs of Addison N. Scurlock*.

9. Scurlock interview, January 24, 1989.

10. Ibid., January 6, 1989; Winston, "Introduction to Washington and the 'Secret City.'"

11. Scurlock interview, January 24, 1989.

12. Trescott, "Love of the People, Control of the Craft."

13. Scurlock interview, January 24, 1989.

14. Trescott, "Love of the People, Control of the Craft."

15. *Washington City Directory*, 1911.

16. Scurlock interview, January 6, 1989.

17. Ibid., January 24, 1989.

18. Ibid.; Trescott, "Love of the People, Control of the Craft." Robert Scurlock's photographs of Italy were featured in a one-man show at Howard University's Gallery of Art in 1947.

19. Scurlock interview, January 24, 1989; Ellsworth Davis, interview with the author, February 10, 1989, Washington, D.C.

20. Scurlock interview, January 6, 1989.

21. Ibid., January 24, 1989; Trescott, "Love of the People, Control of the Craft"; Robert S. Scurlock résumé, in author's possession. Robert Scurlock actually began working with color photography in the late 1940s and established Washington Stock Photo, an agency specializing in classic color views of Washington landmarks. The agency continued to market Washington views worldwide into the 1990s.

22. Trescott, "Love of the People, Control of the Craft."

23. Scurlock interviews, January 6 and 24, 1989; Trescott, "Love of the People, Control of the Craft."

24. Scurlock interview, January 24, 1989; James Haskins, *P. B. S. Pinchback* (New York: Macmillan, 1973), 131–247.

5.1 Robert S. Scurlock, *Fredi Washington,* 1930s. Schomburg Center for Research in Black Culture, New York Public Library.

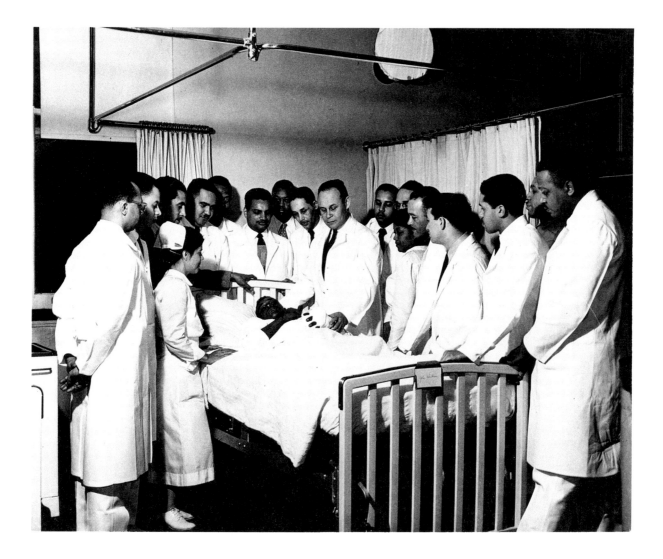

5.2 Scurlock Studio, *Dr. Charles Drew Teaching at Freedmen's (now Howard University) Hospital,* n.d. Prints and Photographs Division, Howard University; courtesy of the Robert S. Scurlock estate, Washington, D.C.

5.3 Robert S. Scurlock, *Marian Anderson*, 1939. Prints and Photographs Division, Howard University; courtesy of the Robert S. Scurlock estate, Washington, D.C.

5.4 Addison N. Scurlock, *Ernest Everett Just*, n.d. Prints and Photographs Division, Howard University; courtesy of the Robert S. Scurlock estate, Washington, D.C.

5.5 Scurlock Studio, *National Association of Republican Women Dinner*, n.d. Georgia Johnson Douglas Collection, Prints and Photographs Division, Howard University; courtesy of the Robert S. Scurlock estate, Washington, D.C.

5.6 Scurlock Studio, *Drawing Class, Howard University,* n.d. The original caption reads: "Another section of the course in Engineering Drawing is Freehand Drawing. This scene, taken in an art studio, shows a group of students doing freehand sketches of mechanical instruments. Granville W. Hurley is the instructor." Prints and Photographs Division, Howard University; courtesy of the Robert S. Scurlock estate, Washington, D.C.

5.7 Scurlock Studio, *Mechanical Drawing Class, Howard University*, n.d. Prints and Photographs Division, Howard University; courtesy of the Robert S. Scurlock estate, Washington, D.C.

5.8 Scurlock Studio, *Board of Trustees, Howard University*, n.d., Prints and Photographs Division, Howard University; courtesy of the Robert S. Scurlock estate, Washington, D.C.

5.9 Scurlock Studio, *Howard University Football Game*, n.d. Prints and Photographs Division, Howard University; courtesy of the Robert S. Scurlock estate, Washington, D.C.

5.10 Scurlock Studio, *Howard University President Mordecai Johnson and Eleanor Roosevelt*, 1940s. The original caption reads: "Mrs. Franklin D. Roosevelt and Dr. Mordecai W. Johnson, president of Howard University, are shown as they pass an ROTC honor guard enroute to the recent special assembly at Howard where Mrs. Roosevelt was the principal speaker. At the Assembly, the former first lady, who is a Trustee at Howard, reiterated her plea for western recognition of the rights of peoples in underdeveloped areas throughout the world." Prints and Photographs Division, Howard University; courtesy of the Robert S. Scurlock estate, Washington, D.C.

5.11 Scurlock Studio, *Howard University Faculty and Board of Trustees*, ca. 1930. Otto McLarin Collection, Prints and Photographs Division, Howard University; courtesy of the Robert S. Scurlock estate, Washington, D.C.

5.12 Scurlock Studio, *ROTC, Howard University*, ca. 1949. Prints and Photographs Division, Howard University; courtesy of the Robert S. Scurlock estate, Washington, D.C.

5.13 Scurlock Studio, *California Club, Union Station*, August 31, 1937. Georgia Fraser Goins Collection, Prints and Photographs Division, Howard University; courtesy of the Robert S. Scurlock estate, Washington, D.C.

5.14 Scurlock Studio, *Sterling Brown*, n.d. Prints and Photographs Division, Howard University; courtesy of the Robert S. Scurlock estate, Washington, D.C.

5.15 Scurlock Studio, *Mrs. Lenora Drew and Her Four Children*, n.d. Charles R. Drew Papers, Prints and Photographs Division, Howard University; courtesy of the Robert S. Scurlock estate, Washington, D.C.

5.16 Robert S. Scurlock, *Drama Coach*, 1948. Courtesy of the Robert S. Scurlock estate, Washington, D.C.

6. FLASHBACK

Gordon Parks and the Image of the Capital City

Deborah Willis

*For me the function of a photographer, I think it's just to report accurately the way we live . . .
our social system, our moods, what we think is ugly, what beautiful. The photographer's job isn't
to change these things; he just shows them up as they are, and the people take it from there.*

—Gordon Parks

Gordon Parks, who called himself "a reporter with a camera," is noted for his direct, realistic style in photographing life in America, particularly during his short tenure as a Farm Security Administration (FSA) photographer. Born in Fort Scott, Kansas, on November 30, 1912, Parks was the youngest of fifteen children. He lived an extraordinary life before 1950. As a teenager, he worked as a cow-puncher and played cornet in the school orchestra; and he was at various times a waiter, a porter, a piano player in night clubs, before he became a photographer.

After his mother's death, when he was sixteen, Parks left Kansas for Minneapolis to live with an older, married sister. He found a job as a waiter on the Northern Pacific Railroad, which traveled from Minneapolis–St. Paul to Seattle via Chicago. Riding the rails was lucrative and inspiring. He wrote musical compositions and read voraciously. "On quieter runs," he says, "in between meals, when the wealthy passengers were either sleeping or consuming alcohol in the lounge cars, I read every magazine I could get my hands on."[1] From 1935 to 1943, photographers hired by the FSA (one of President Franklin Delano Roosevelt's New Deal programs) traveled the country photographing rural and urban America. The admiration and courage of the work produced by these photographers convinced Parks, that he, too, should become a photographer.

The photographers he studied were Ben Shahn, Jack Delano, Carl Mydans, Dorothea Lange, John Vachon, and Walker Evans. "They were photographing poverty, and I knew poverty so well," Parks recalls. "They were covering Okies in California. It was the Steinbeck era." He goes on:

> In one [magazine] that had been left behind by a passenger I found a portfolio of photographs that I would never forget. They were of migrant workers. Dispossessed, beaten by storms, dust and floods, they roamed the highways in caravans of battered jalopies and wagons between Oklahoma and California, scrounging for work. Some were so poor that they traveled on foot, pushing their young in baby buggies and carts. They lived in shanties with siding and roofs of cardboard boxes, the inside walls dressed with newspapers. There was a man with two children running through a dust storm to their shanty. . . . These stark, tragic images of human beings caught up in the confusion of poverty saddened me. I took the magazine home and studied it for weeks. Meanwhile I read John Steinbeck's *In Dubious Battle* and Erskine Caldwell and Margaret Bourke-White's *You Have Seen Their Faces.* These books stayed in my mind.[2]

Within weeks of studying the images in the periodical he found on the train, Parks bought his first camera, a Voightlander Brilliant, at a pawnshop for $7.50. He states that this first purchase was "[n]ot much of a camera, but a great name to toss around. I had bought what was to become my weapon against poverty and racism."[3]

Parks, by then married with a child, began to dream and to critically assess his future as a porter on the train. Despite his extended trips away from his family, the long layovers in Chicago, and the nature of his job, he fulfilled his diligent quest to understand and explore his creative urges. His passion led him to visit the Art Institute of Chicago, "spending hours in this large voiceless place, studying paintings of Monet, Renoir and Manet."[4] He also visited the Southside Community Art Center, dubbed the unofficial auxiliary of the art institute. There he met Charles White, the noted black artist who lived in Chicago during this period. White described his own work as taking

> shape around images and ideas that are centered within the vortex of the life experience of a Negro. . . .
> I look to life and to my people as the founthead [sic] of challenging ideas and monumental concepts. . . .

> I look for security in alliance with the millions of artists throughout the world with whom I share common goals. And I look to all mankind to communicate with and to appropriate my works.[5]

There is no doubt in this writer's mind that the experiences Parks embarked upon during his layovers in Chicago—such as his interaction with White and other artists at the Southside Community Art Center—brought a new consciousness to the artist's own passion to create art. Parks expresses the impact of White's work on his photographic vision in this way:

> There were a number of talented young people who worked at the Center during those days, and one of the most promising was Charles White, a painter. He was mild-appearing, bespectacled, and blessed with humor, but his powerful, black figures pointed at the kind of photography that I knew I should be doing. . . . It was good to laugh and talk with him; and it was good to watch him strengthen an arm with a delicate brush stroke or give anguish to a face with mixtures of coloring. We had great hopes.[6]

Parks recalls the details of this period with great nostalgia.

> The first few rolls I had taken with [my new camera] were earning respect from the Eastman Kodak Company. The manager of its Minneapolis branch showed surprise when he found out they were my very first attempt, and he emphatically assured me that they were very good. Too, he promised me a showing in their window gallery if I kept progressing. Dubious, I thanked him, smiled and told him I would hold him to his promise. After that hardly a thing faced my Voightlander that I didn't attempt to glorify—sunsets, beaches, boats, skies, even an elaborate pattern of pigeon droppings on the courthouse steps. I wasn't rushing to the bank with proceeds from those first efforts but experience was mounting, giving me a sense of direction. The gentleman at Eastman lived up to his promise; six months later he had my photographs placed in the company's show windows.[7]

He later found the images he made of the waterfront insignificant and turned his camera on a new subject. "Natural instinct had served to aim my sights much higher, and those Farm Security photographs with all their power were still pushing my thoughts around," he says.

> Before long I had deserted the waterfronts, skyscrapers and canals for Chicago's south side—the city's sprawling impoverished black belt. And there among the squalid, rickety tenements that housed the poor, a new way of seeing and feeling opened up to me. A photograph I made of an ill-dressed black

child wandering in a trash-littered alley and another of two aged men warming themselves at a bonfire during a heavy snowfall pleased me more than any I had made. They convinced me that even the cheap camera I had bought was capable of making a serious comment on the human condition. Subconsciously I was moving toward the documentary field, and Chicago's south side was a remarkably pitiful place to start. The worst of it was like bruises on the face of humanity.[8]

Captivated by documentary photography, Parks found it necessary to spend more time in Chicago. "I increased my visits to Chicago and to its Southside Art Center which sat formidably in the heart of the black belt," he recalls.

Once a stately mansion owned by the rich, it was now a haven for struggling black artists, sculptors and writers. The gallery walls were usually weighted with the work of well-known painters who used their art to encourage protest from the underprivileged and dispossessed. How effective they were remains questionable, but for me, at the time, their approach to art seemed commensurate with the people they were attempting to serve.[9]

Undoubtedly, Parks had become enraptured with photography. The artist was maturing; he could see the photograph not only as poetic rendering but also as lyrical musing. He looked for inspiration from art that evoked compassion for the subjects portrayed. "On exhibit inside [the center] were the works of Soyer, Charles White, Ben Shahn, Max Weber and Alexander Brook, along with the merciless satires of William Gropper and Jack Levine," he recalls.

Oppression was their subject matter. With paint, pencil and charcoal, they had put down on canvas what they had seen, and what they had felt about it. Quite forcefully they were showing me that art could be most effective in expressing discontent, while suggesting that the camera—in the right hands—could do the same. They had forsaken the lovely pink ladies of Manet and Renoir, the soft bluish-green landscapes of Monet that hung several miles north at Chicago's Art Institute. To me these classicists were painters who told far different tales, and for several weeks the difference between the two schools—one classical, the other harshly documentary—would expand the possibilities of the artistic directions I could take.[10]

An award from the Julius Rosenwald Fund in 1941 provided Parks with a renewed enthusiasm for his art. One weekday afternoon, when Parks was visiting the center, Charles White told him about the fund. Despondent because he had not yet received a fellowship, White suggested that they both apply for one. Parks enthusiastically agreed. He decided to photograph life on the south side of Chicago and use that work to apply for the fellowship. Using his poetic approach of documenting and interpreting poverty, he began the project that would ultimately transform his life. "That Saturday morning I started poking around the south side with my camera, I knew that more than anything else I wanted to strike at the evil of poverty. . . . My own brush with it was motive enough, yet this landscape of ash piles, garbage heaps, tired tenements and littered streets was worse than any I had seen."[11] Parks photographed the perpetual reality of poverty. He recorded funerals, church services, families, gamblers, police brutality, and the desperate lives of the children who lived in the area. He wrote to art historian and philosopher Alain Locke, writer Horace Cayton, and the center's director, Peter Pollack, requesting letters of support for the Julius Rosenwald Fellowship. Pollack and his staff organized an exhibition of the photographs Parks had made, including his landscapes and the south side images.

Reflectively, Parks writes: "During that first year there [in Chicago] my family learned to spell 'suffer.' But just when food and money hit the zero mark, fate resurrected my hopes. . . . Writers painters, sculptors and scholars had been recipients of fellowships—but never a photographer."[12] Initially rejected by the first group of jurors, who were all white, well-established photographers, Parks's photographs received a reprieve when they were reviewed by another jury composed of painters and sculptors. In December of 1941, Parks received notice that he was the first photographer to receive a Rosenwald fellowship. It was a historic time. December was the month that Pearl Harbor was attacked; 1941 was the year that Richard Wright wrote *Twelve Million Black Voices*, using FSA photographs to examine the plight of black life. Its style and premise were similar to Caldwell and Bourke-White's *You Have Seen Their Faces*. The fellowship was for two hundred dollars a month. Parks chose to work with Roy Stryker at the Farm Security Administration.

He joined the FSA in January 1942. "I was to serve out my fellowship with the Farm Security Administration with those same photographers whose work had beckoned to me when I was a waiter on the North Coast Limited. It was an extravagant moment as we began packing, and for the next two years Washington, D.C., would be our home."[13]

Parks received extensive training as a photojournalist under Roy Stryker's direction. He describes with candor and respect the advice he received from his mentor. "I learned a lot from Stryker. He wasn't a photographer himself but he knew which way the camera should be pointed. He made me look at the camera as a very purposeful instrument . . . it became the weapon to speak against anything we disliked in the world of fact."[14]

Filled with exuberance and apprehension about this new city, Parks expresses his initial feelings toward Washington, D.C.

> I arrived there in January of that year with scant knowledge of the place. . . . Sensing this, Roy Stryker, sent me out to get acquainted with the rituals of the nation's capital. I went in a hurry and with enthusiasm. . . . My contentment was short-lived. Within the hour the day began opening up like a bad dream; even here in this radiant, high-hearted place racism was busy with its dirty work. Eating houses shooed me to the back door; theatres refused me a seat.[15]

His past memories of racism, poverty, and deprivation came back in one single afternoon. The insults he received at Garfinckel's department store and the insensitivity of the whites he encountered in the city embittered him. Parks regarded all racial insults as personal affronts. "It suddenly seemed that all of America was finding grim pleasure in expressing its intolerance to me personally. Washington had turned ugly, and my angry past came back to speak with me as I walked along, assuring me that, even here in the nation's capital, the walls of bigotry and discrimination stood high and formidable."[16]

Returning to the FSA offices, Parks met with Stryker, who informed him that he was concerned about the photographer being able to cope with the racism of the nation's capital. Stryker declared, "As for that city out there, well—it's been here for a long time, full of bigotry and hatred for black people. You brought a camera to town with you. If you use it intelligently, you might help turn things around. It's a powerful instrument in the right hands." Stryker went on to say:

> Obviously you ran into some bigots out there this afternoon. Well, its not enough to photograph one of them and label his photograph "bigot." Bigots have a way of looking like everyone else. You have to get at the source of their bigotry. And that's not easy. That's what you'll have to work at, and that's why I took you on. Read. Read a lot. Talk to other black people who have spent their lives here. They might help to give you some direction.[17]

Having spent only a few days in Washington, and with a curious combination of training in photography and literary inspiration,[18] Parks took a photograph that is now known as his signature image, one of the first he took in the capital—*American Gothic*. It is of an African American cleaning woman in a government office building; Roy Stryker had suggested that the photographer speak with her and find out her views on life. Parks spent a great deal of time with her, photographing her at work and at home, and developed a masterful photographic essay about Ella Watson, the cleaning woman. He later commented:

> What the camera had to do was expose the evils of racism, the evils of poverty, the discrimination and the bigotry, by showing the people who suffered most under it. . . . The photograph of the black cleaning woman standing in front of the American flag with a broom and a mop expressed more than any other photograph I have taken. It was the first one I took in Washington, D.C. I thought then, and Roy Stryker eventually proved it to me, that you could not photograph a person who turns you away from the motion picture ticket window, or someone who refuses to feed you, or someone who refuses to wait on you in a store. You could not photograph him and say "This is a bigot."[19]

It is the facial expressions in Parks's photographs that tell the story—of hard work and hardship, of the struggle of people's daily lives—whether the subject is a cleaning woman or an old street vendor, a construction worker or a panhandler, or children in the doorway of their home. He captures them in what is seemingly an unguarded moment. In looking at *American Gothic*, I am reminded of Langston Hughes's concept of "the dream deferred." Parks's image is about second-class citizenship, the disinherited.

Parks's documentation of the peculiar quality of life of blacks living in the nation's capital, represented in the images following this essay, reveals a strikingly different manner from that of the African American studio and journalistic photographers who thrived in Washington, D.C., during the 1930s and 1940s. The studio and newspaper photographers documented the world of the upper and middle classes: weddings, cotillions, annual dinners. Parks looked at the social implications of the underemployed and their children; he made thought-provoking images of the disenfranchised. Stylistically, he became adept at fusing the artistic with the journalistic. As Nicholas Natanson so aptly states, "Parks does not stint on irony."[20]

The racial and social implications of Parks's photography are apparent in his images of the family of Ella Watson. In one of Parks's more subtle photographs, in which a young black girl holds a white doll, he begins to suggest the identity struggle that points to the African American self-image and how much it has been defined by the values and standards of the larger culture. Parks's photographs of the young girl and her grandmother, who might have purchased the doll, challenge the idea of material fulfillment—which results in the loss of self.

Parks, like the other documentary photographers of the FSA, created politicized images of the social conditions of the underemployed. Simply put, his photographs define African Americans in relationship to the "owning" class, the have-nots and the haves. His suggestive imagery of the black community as a colonial outpost in the shadow of the Capitol dome mirrors the writings of Richard Wright in *Twelve Million Black Voices*. Wright states:

> The seasons of the plantation no longer dictate the lives of many of us; hundreds of thousands of us are moving into the sphere of conscious history. . . . We are with the new tide. We stand at the crossroads. We watch each new procession. The hot wires carry urgent appeals. Print compels us. Voices are speaking. Men are moving! And we shall be with them.[21]

Parks recorded the dramatic duality of life in Washington, D.C. The key to understanding Parks's images lies in a description of the social history of the capital at this time.

> Whereas the population of all but eight or nine American cities declined during the decade, Washington's increased by 36 percent. Before midsummer of 1940, the number of federal employees in the city had risen to about 166,000. Colored businessmen had little stake in this mounting prosperity. Although the nearly 42 percent increase in the Negro population outstripped the 34 percent white increase, Negro purchasing power rose relatively little, if at all, during the decade. . . . The building trades unions, the bulwark of organized labor in Washington, kept [African Americans] out of skilled construction jobs, and hopes that the Capital Transit Company would hire Negro platform workers collapsed when the Transit Union threatened a walkout if a single Negro were employed. Year after year, moreover, an unrecorded number of practically destitute Negro families arrived from the Southern states to swell the District's unskilled labor supply.[22]

This description of Washington is important, as it distinguishes the subjects Parks photographed. Equipped with a sensitivity toward poverty, Parks provided poor families and the unemployed with visual empowerment. The interior of Ella Watson's home reflects her sense of family and religion. A framed photographic portrait of a well-dressed couple is placed prominently on her dresser. The photograph, possibly of Mrs. Watson prior to her husband's death, is somewhat anecdotal.[23] The composition shows the scarcity of treasured possessions in Mrs. Watson's life; all she has are the photograph and her grandchildren. The reflection of Mrs. Watson's adopted daughter is seen in the mirror's surface. As accomplished as this photograph is in telling her family story, another of Parks's photographs also dramatically represents how important religion was to Ella Watson; there is an "altar" with religious icons on another dresser. Mrs. Watson and her adopted daughter look as though they are in deep thought as the viewer's gaze is transfixed on the symbolic statuary figures, which include a crucifix, rosary, and two elephants. The mystical fusion of religious and allegorical good luck figures creates a wonderful paradox.

To contrast the images of Mrs. Watson's home, Parks walked the streets of the District, traveling through southwest, southeast, and northwest. His images demonstrate that he was not static. Two undeniably distinctive Parks photographs of the contrasting housing situation in Washington create a curious tension. In one image two young boys stand on a hilltop overlooking the newly built housing project, Frederick Douglass Dwellings. The photograph creates a sense of hope and a possibility of dreams fulfilled by these new houses. The housing project on Alabama Avenue in the southeast included 313 four- and six-room units. The image of it includes two young boys in the foreground shooting marbles. The photographer captures the young boys at play, oblivious to the awkward structures in the background—the façades of their homes. Questions naturally arise about the romanticized nature of both photographs: the photographer has combined the real with the surreal.

There was much controversy in the building of public housing in Washington, D.C. A local newspaper description of the Frederick Douglass Dwellings, noting the differentiations made for blacks and whites in the segregated housing policy, reads:

> . . . units for colored occupancy, completed by National Capital Housing Authority in 1941. Frame and masonry construction, no basements, baths not tile, equipped with space heaters instead of central heating. Cost, excluding land, $1,089 a room. . . . East Capitol street houses—108 units for white occupancy, three and one-half to four rooms, completed in 1943 by Davy & Murphy, private builders. Brick construction, basement, central heating and tile baths. Cost, including land, $896, per room.[24]

Through his photographs, Parks "highlight[ed] the amenities of the spanking new Frederick Douglass housing project, at the same time he made a visual tour of the dingy houses, littered yards, unsightly privies . . . housed near the nation's capitol."[25]

Commenting on Parks's approach to photographing his subjects, photographer Robert H. McNeill states:

> I remember seeing him covering a Howard University commencement, and even the other black photographers who were there were saying, "Who is that crazy [guy]?" I mean, Gordon would use four

flashbulbs for a single shot, outdoors where he could have gotten away without using any. He wasn't content just to stand up and take shots from a position that was comfortable for him—he lay on the ground, he shot up, he shot down. He was more like a movie director, trying to capture the whole academic atmosphere.[26]

During World War II, Parks worked for the Office of War Information (OWI) as a correspondent. He was assigned to document life in wartime Washington and photograph the black airmen stationed in Sheffield, Michigan. He later became a photojournalist with the Standard Oil Company in New Jersey, again under the direction of Roy Stryker, photographing the "face" of America, its problems and its people. In 1949, Parks became a staff photographer for *Life* magazine and was active covering stories of interest to black and white America.

The importance of Gordon Parks's work to the genre of documentary photography is surely beyond question. It is Parks's own documentation and analysis of the historical struggles of black people that authenticate his photographs. The challenge he presented to Roy Stryker and his colleagues resulted in a broader reading into the works produced by the FSA and OWI photographers, as Parks transformed his subjects and their plight by allowing the viewer to consider the different messages presented in the New Deal photography programs.

Notes

1. Gordon Parks, *Voices in the Mirror: An Autobiography* (New York: Doubleday, 1990), p. 65.
2. Ibid.
3. Ibid., p. 66.
4. Ibid., p. 74.
5. Cedric Dover, *American Negro Art* (New York: New York Graphic Society, 1960), p. 49.
6. Gordon Parks, *A Choice of Weapons* (New York: Perennial Library, Harper and Row, 1973), p. 171.
7. Parks, *Voices in the Mirror*, p. 74.
8. Ibid.
9. Ibid., p. 75.
10. Ibid.
11. Parks, *A Choice of Weapons*, p. 172.
12. Parks, *Voices in the Mirror*, p. 78.
13. Ibid., p. 79.
14. Howard Chapnick, *Truth Needs No Ally: Inside Photojournalism* (Columbia: University of Missouri, 1994), p. 135.

15. Parks, *Voices in the Mirror*, p. 81.

16. Ibid., p. 82.

17. Ibid.

18. Parks was self-taught and his work was largely informed by the writings of the period. He notes that "recognizing more than ever the necessity for knowledge, I threw myself into stacks of books, trying to couple my visual sense with the theme of the more significant writers. Richard Wright's *Twelve Million Black Voices* became my bible" (*A Choice of Weapons*, p. 190).

19. Martin H. Bush, *The Photographs of Gordon Parks* (Wichita, Kans.: Ulrich Museum of Art, Wichita State University, 1983), p. 38.

20. Barbara Orbach and Nicholas Natanson, "The Mirror Image: Black Washington in World War II–Era Federal Photography," in *Washington History* 4, no. 1 (spring/summer 1992): p. 18.

21. Richard Wright, *Twelve Million Black Voices* (New York: Arno Press, 1969).

22. Constance McLaughlin Green, *The Secret City: A History of Race Relations in the Nation's Capital* (Princeton, N.J.: Princeton University Press, 1967), p. 228.

23. Parks interviewed Ella Watson before photographing her and discovered that "she had struggled alone after her mother had died and her father had been killed by a lynch mob. She had gone through high school, married, and become pregnant. Her husband was accidentally shot to death two days before the daughter was born. By the time the daughter was 18 she had given birth to two illegitimate children, dying two weeks after the second child's birth. What's more, the first child had been stricken with paralysis a year before its mother died. Now this woman was bringing up these grandchildren on a salary hardly suitable for one person" (*A Choice of Weapons*, p. 188).

24. W. E. Washington, in "Urban Redevelopment in the District," *Washington Tribune*, September 21, 1946. The years 1942 to 1946 constituted a turbulent period in the development of government-subsidized housing structures. The Frederick Douglass complex was at the center of controversy between advocates and opponents of public housing. In 1944, the Federation of Citizens Association charged the National Capital Housing Authority, before the Senate District Committee on Housing, with creating public housing that cost more than comparable dwellings in private enterprise. The adoption of the District of Columbia Redevelopment Act (PL 592) was in large part due to the discussions following the Senate committee hearings of 1944, as noted by Washington.

25. Orbach and Natanson, "The Mirror Image," pp. 15–16.

26. Nicholas Natanson, *The Black Image in the New Deal: The Politics of FSA Photography* (Knoxville: University of Tennessee Press, 1992), p. 266.

6.1 Morgan and Marvin Smith, *Gordon Parks, Posing with Camera*, ca. 1946. Schomburg Center for Research in Black Culture, New York Public Library.

6.2 Gordon Parks, *American Gothic*, August 1942, Washington, D.C. Courtesy of Gordon Parks.

6.3 Gordon Parks, *Mrs. Ella Watson, a Government Charwoman, with Three Grandchildren and Her Adopted Daughter*, August 1942, Washington, D.C. Library of Congress, U.S. Department of Agriculture Farm Security Administration files, LC-USF 34-13432-C.

6.4 Gordon Parks, *Mrs. Ella Watson, a Government Charwoman, Leaves for Work at 4:30 P.M.*, August 1942, Washington, D.C. Library of Congress, U.S. Department of Agriculture Farm Security Administration files, LC-USF 34-13438-C.

6.5 Gordon Parks, *Neighborhood Children* (Ella Watson's grandchildren), November 1942, Washington, D.C. (southwest section). Library of Congress, U.S. Office of War Information files, LC-USW 3-11074-C.

6.6 Gordon Parks, *An Old Peanut Vendor on Seaton Road*, June 1942, Washington, D.C. Library of Congress, U.S. Department of Agriculture Farm Security Administration files, LC-USF 34-13309-C.

6.7 Gordon Parks, *Construction Workman*, June 1942, Washington, D.C. Library of Congress, U.S. Department of Agriculture Farm Security Administration files, LC-USF 34-13352-C.

6.8 Gordon Parks, *Waterfront Fruit Market*, November 1942, Washington, D.C. Library of Congress, U.S. Office of War Information files, LC-USW 3-10705-E.

6.9 Gordon Parks, *Mr. and Mrs. Venus Alsobrook in Front of Their Home in the Southwest Section. Mr. Alsobrook Is an Official Salvage Collector for the Government*, November 1942, Washington, D.C. Library of Congress, U.S. Office of War Information files, LC-USW 3-10708-C.

6.10 Gordon Parks, *A Mother Preparing Dinner in a One-Room Flat,* November 1942, Washington, D.C. (southwest section). Library of Congress, U.S. Office of War Information files, LC-USW 3-11049-C.

6.11 Gordon Parks, *Woman Washing Clothes in Her Kitchen*, November 1942, Washington, D.C. (southwest section). Library of Congress, U.S. Office of War Information files, LC-USW 3-11058-C.

6.12 Gordon Parks, *Two Brothers in a One-Room Flat*, November 1942, Washington, D.C. (southwest section). Library of Congress, U.S. Office of War Information files, LC-USW 3-11052-C.

6.13 Gordon Parks, *Frederick Douglass Housing Project. Boys Overlooking the Project*, July 1942, Anacostia, Washington, D.C. Library of Congress, U.S. Department of Agriculture Farm Security Administration files, LC-USF 34-13368-C.

6.14 Gordon Parks, *Two Boys Shooting Marbles in Front of Their Homes*, November 1942, Washington, D.C. (southwest section). Library of Congress, U.S. Department of Agriculture Farm Security Administration files, LC-USF 3-11050-C.

6.15 Gordon Parks, *Boys Playing Leapfrog Near the Frederick Douglass Project*, July 1942, Washington, D.C. Library of Congress, U.S. Department of Agriculture Farm Security Administration files, LC-USF 34-13882-C.

6.16 Gordon Parks, *Apartment House at 1739 Seaton Road*, June 1942, Washington, D.C. Library of Congress, U.S. Department of Agriculture Farm Security Administration files, LC-USF 34-13303-C.

6.17 Gordon Parks, *Frederick Douglass Housing Project. Playing in the Community Sprayer,* July 1942, Anacostia, Washington, D.C. Library of Congress, U.S. Department of Agriculture Farm Security Administration files, LC-USF 34-13370-C.

6.18 Gordon Parks, *Saturday Afternoon, 7th Street and Florida Avenue, NW*, August 1942, Washington, D.C. Library of Congress, U.S. Department of Agriculture Farm Security Administration files, LC-USF 34-13448-C.

6.19 Gordon Parks, *Soldiers and Civilians at the Information Desk at the Union Station*, November 1942, Washington, D.C. Library of Congress, U.S. Office of War Information files, LC-USW 3-12121-C.

6.20 Gordon Parks, *Interior View of the Union Station with Office of War Information Poster in the Background,* March 1943, Washington, D.C. Library of Congress, U.S. Office of War Information files, LC-USW 3-18393-C.

6.21 Gordon Parks, *Crowds of Soldiers, Sailors, and Civilians Waiting to Board Trains at Union Station*, December 1942, Washington, D.C. Library of Congress, U.S. Office of War Information files, LC-USW 3-12125-C.

CONTRIBUTORS

Jane Freundel Levey, editor of *Washington History*, the journal of the Historical Society of Washington, D.C., regularly consulted with Robert S. Scurlock on photography research projects until his death in 1994. She has extensive experience as a photo researcher, writer, editor, and historian. She recently edited *At Peace with All Their Neighbors: Catholics and Catholicism in Washington, D.C.*, by William W. Warner (1994).

Jane Lusaka, formerly a writer and editor for the Smithsonian Institution's Center for African American History and Culture, is an associate editor at the American Association of Museums. She was a photo researcher for *The African Americans* (1993) and was a contributor to the *Encyclopedia of African American Culture and History* (1996), edited by Jack Salzman, David Lionel Smith, and Cornel West. She has written several articles about the work of African American artists and photographers, and interviewed Robert McNeill about his life and work in 1993 and 1995.

Nicholas Natanson, an archivist in the Still Picture Branch of the National Archives, is the author of *The Black Image in the New Deal: The Politics of FSA Photography, 1935–1943* (1992) and an article about Robert H. McNeill's Virginia photographs for the British journal *History of Photography* (Spring 1995).

Melissa Rachleff, a photography historian and curator, interviewed both Marvin and Morgan Smith for her master's thesis while a graduate student at New York University. In 1993 she curated *Images of Harlem, 1935–1952*, an exhibition of photographs by the Smiths for the University of Kentucky Art Museum in Lexington, Kentucky. She is currently working as the assistant curator at Exit Art in New York.

Deborah Willis, curator of exhibitions for the Smithsonian Institution's Center for African American History and Culture, is an art photographer and a historian and curator of African American photography and culture. She is the editor of *Picturing Us: African American Identity in Photography* and *Imagining Families: Images and Voices* (both 1994), and the author of *VanDerZee: The Portraits of James VanDerZee* and *J. P. Ball: Daguerrean and Studio Photographer* (both 1993), *Lorna Simpson* (1992), *Black Photographers, 1940–1988: An Illustrated Bio-Bibliography* (1988), and *Black Photographers, 1840–1940: An Illustrated Bio-Bibliography* (1985).